IMPROVING PROFIT

USING CONTRIBUTION METRICS TO BOOST THE BOTTOM LINE

Keith N. Cleland

apress®

Improving Profit: Using Contribution Metrics to Boost the Bottom Line

Copyright © 2013 by **Keith N. Cleland**

This work is subject to copyright. All rights are reserved by the Publisher, whether the whole or part of the material is concerned, specifically the rights of translation, reprinting, reuse of illustrations, recitation, broadcasting, reproduction on microfilms or in any other physical way, and transmission or information storage and retrieval, electronic adaptation, computer software, or by similar or dissimilar methodology now known or hereafter developed. Exempted from this legal reservation are brief excerpts in connection with reviews or scholarly analysis or material supplied specifically for the purpose of being entered and executed on a computer system, for exclusive use by the purchaser of the work. Duplication of this publication or parts thereof is permitted only under the provisions of the Copyright Law of the Publisher's location, in its current version, and permission for use must always be obtained from Springer. Permissions for use may be obtained through RightsLink at the Copyright Clearance Center. Violations are liable to prosecution under the respective Copyright Law.

ISBN-13 (pbk): 978-1-4302-6307-4

ISBN-13 (electronic): 978-1-4302-6308-1

Trademarked names, logos, and images may appear in this book. Rather than use a trademark symbol with every occurrence of a trademarked name, logo, or image we use the names, logos, and images only in an editorial fashion and to the benefit of the trademark owner, with no intention of infringement of the trademark.

The use in this publication of trade names, trademarks, service marks, and similar terms, even if they are not identified as such, is not to be taken as an expression of opinion as to whether or not they are subject to proprietary rights.

While the advice and information in this book are believed to be true and accurate at the date of publication, neither the authors nor the editors nor the publisher can accept any legal responsibility for any errors or omissions that may be made. The publisher makes no warranty, express or implied, with respect to the material contained herein.

President and Publisher: Paul Manning
Acquisitions Editor: Jeff Olson
Editorial Board: Steve Anglin, Mark Beckner, Ewan Buckingham, Gary Cornell, Louise Corrigan,
    Jonathan Gennick, Jonathan Hassell, Robert Hutchinson, Michelle Lowman,
    James Markham, Matthew Moodie, Jeff Olson, Jeffrey Pepper, Douglas Pundick,
    Ben Renow-Clarke, Dominic Shakeshaft, Gwenan Spearing, Matt Wade, Tom Welsh
Coordinating Editor: Rita Fernando
Copy Editor: James Fraleigh
Compositor: SPi Global
Indexer: SPi Global
Cover Designer: Anna Ishchenko

Distributed to the book trade worldwide by Springer Science+Business Media New York, 233 Spring Street, 6th Floor, New York, NY 10013. Phone 1-800-SPRINGER, fax (201) 348-4505, e-mail orders-ny@springer-sbm.com, or visit www.springeronline.com. Apress Media, LLC is a California LLC and the sole member (owner) is Springer Science + Business Media Finance Inc (SSBM Finance Inc). SSBM Finance Inc is a Delaware corporation.

For information on translations, please e-mail rights@apress.com, or visit www.apress.com.

Apress and friends of ED books may be purchased in bulk for academic, corporate, or promotional use. eBook versions and licenses are also available for most titles. For more information, reference our Special Bulk Sales–eBook Licensing web page at www.apress.com/bulk-sales.

Any source code or other supplementary materials referenced by the author in this text is available to readers at www.apress.com. For detailed information about how to locate your book's source code, go to www.apress.com/source-code/.

Apress Business: The Unbiased Source of Business Information

Apress business books provide essential information and practical advice, each written for practitioners by recognized experts. Busy managers and professionals in all areas of the business world—and at all levels of technical sophistication—look to our books for the actionable ideas and tools they need to solve problems, update and enhance their professional skills, make their work lives easier, and capitalize on opportunity.

Whatever the topic on the business spectrum—entrepreneurship, finance, sales, marketing, management, regulation, information technology, among others—Apress has been praised for providing the objective information and unbiased advice you need to excel in your daily work life. Our authors have no axes to grind; they understand they have one job only—to deliver up-to-date, accurate information simply, concisely, and with deep insight that addresses the real needs of our readers.

It is increasingly hard to find information—whether in the news media, on the Internet, and now all too often in books—that is even-handed and has your best interests at heart. We therefore hope that you enjoy this book, which has been carefully crafted to meet our standards of quality and unbiased coverage.

We are always interested in your feedback or ideas for new titles. Perhaps you'd even like to write a book yourself. Whatever the case, reach out to us at editorial@apress.com and an editor will respond swiftly. Incidentally, at the back of this book, you will find a list of useful related titles. Please visit us at www.apress.com to sign up for newsletters and discounts on future purchases.

The Apress Business Team

This book is dedicated to my wife Carolyn, without whose love, patience, and prayerful support, along with Paul and Suzy's belief that the concepts in this book are "awesomely simple" and should be made known to businesses everywhere, it is unlikely this book would have been written.

Contents

Foreword ix
About the Author. xi
Acknowledgments xiii
Introduction xv

Chapter 1: Background to Contribution-Based Activity (CBA) 1
Chapter 2: Kitchen Utensil Manufacturer Taken to the Cleaners. 11
Chapter 3: Printing Business Multiplies Net Profit by 500%. 17
Chapter 4: Furniture Manufacturer Climbs Out of the Red. 25
Chapter 5: Contractor Overcomes Competition to Make a Profit . . . 33
Chapter 6: Horticultural Equipment Proprietor's
Moment of Truth. 39
Chapter 7: Wholesaler Nets $2.5M in 10+ Months. 49
Chapter 8: Jeweler's Changed Focus Turns Red into Black. 55
Chapter 9: Upmarket Café Learns How to Stay on Track 63
Chapter 10: Diesel Repair Shop Rescued from
Sand-Up- Hill Country. 69
Chapter 11: Garment Maker Multiplies Net Profit by 700%. 75
Chapter 12: Switchboard Manufacturer Climbs into the Black. 83
Chapter 13: Baker Identifies Where the Rubber Meets the Road 91
Chapter 14: Architectural Practice Eradicates a Malignant Cancer. . . 101
Chapter 15: Accounting Firm Wins by Losing a Third of Its Fees. 107
Chapter 16: Legal Firm Transfers Productivity to the Bottom Line. . . 113
Chapter 17: Contractor Increases Strike Rate to 1 in 4 121
Chapter 18: Hot Bread Baker Discovers More to
Bread than Flour. 127
Chapter 19: Window Manufacturer's Flawed Foundation 135
Chapter 20: Multi-Home Contractor Discovers a New Way Home. . . 141

Contents

Chapter 21: Award-Winning Hairdressing Salon
Cuts Its Way Out of Bankruptcy 149
Chapter 22: Multi-Department Store Whitewashes the Past 155
Chapter 23: 14 Businesses Explore CBA/TARI 163
Appendix A: Questions Answered 193
Appendix B: Fast-Track Problem Resolution Guide 205
Appendix C: Definition of Terms 207
Appendix D: The Business Wheel 209
Epilogue: Why Contribution Metrics? 213

Index 217

Foreword

I first met Keith when he was delivering a seminar on his approach to improving business performance, which is the subject of this book. I was interested by his claim that you could manage a business by focusing on two key levers, which, if correctly identified, could help you steer the business to growth and prosperity.

I had by that time been instrumental in improving the performance of many blue chip companies while working for a leading international business consultancy group. As a result, it seemed clear to me that improving business performance was not entirely straightforward and required the knowledge and experience of the complete range of functional and process management disciplines, which I had acquired over the years.

I found his concepts interesting, but, like many people who are first introduced to this approach, I did not really grasp the underlying principles, and so concluded it was too simplistic to have any meaningful application in my world of business (where I believed the problems were much more complex and thereby required more sophisticated solutions).

It was about a year later that our paths crossed again while he was working in the UK, applying his ideas. He persuaded me that if you could create the right focus in business, develop an expectation of success, and create a simple plan that linked activity to financials, this would in itself deliver significant improvement in profitability. I agreed to try his concepts on the business I was currently consulting, even though I was incredulous at his claims of the scale of improvement.

Over the next few weeks, Keith would constantly remind me about TARI, saying, "Just trust me and follow the process and you will see the profit improvement you seek." This was an act of faith, as this process was so different from the well-established approaches to business improvement that had delivered so much success for my colleagues and me.

What I experienced was a revelation. The owner, who had low aspirations and a lack of direction, saw his business transformed in less than a year into a dynamic operation with a growth in profitability I would only expect to see in a Disney movie. I became a firm believer in Keith's concepts, but surprised it had taken me so long to grasp such an obvious truth. Even then I was not convinced the concepts would work in larger organizations.

Foreword

Sometime later, I was consulting with a much larger business that was losing money and ridden with debt. We were working on many issues that needed to be resolved. One evening, while I was discussing the issues over a glass of wine with Keith, he suggested I apply his concepts to this company. I was skeptical whether we would get much benefit for the effort we would need to invest in this larger and more sophisticated organization, although I could see merit in doing some product analysis.

The journey that followed was different from what I had expected. What I had not realized was that the ability of the various departmental managers to contribute was being clouded by their functional performance measures and the opaqueness of costing and financial systems. (This was not the first time I had come across senior business managers who could not relate the profits on a financial statement to their own activities.) What was more, the company's workers at all levels down to the shop floor wanted the company to survive, but did not have the focus or the understanding of how they could contribute to making the company a success.

Keith's concepts provided the company with this much-needed focus and empowered the organization very quickly. Sales and production worked on business activity levels; designers redesigned product with marketing using the added-value-per-hour concept; sales became much more effective in managing product margins; shop floor operators could directly relate their efforts to the company's profitability; and managers had a simple and understandable way of driving the business forward that related their efforts to the profitability of the business. In three years, the debts were cleared and the company was making healthy operating profits.

I believe Keith's work will one day be regarded as a landmark contribution to business owners and managers around the world. I encourage you to read this book, and I hope that you will find the success that I have found by applying Keith's concepts to your organization.

Ronen Day
September 2013

Ronen Day is the Managing Director of the UK division of Fine Tubes Ltd., a company with plants in Plymouth, UK, and New York, USA. He has spent most of his career successfully improving business performance at a senior-management level in industry and with PA Consulting Group, a leading International Management Consultancy. He is a Chartered Engineer with a Master's in Business Administration from London Business School.

About the Author

The author of two books and a dozen articles, **Keith N. Cleland** is currently professor and head of the Financial Management Department, IBR School of Executive Management, at Steinbeis University in Berlin.

Dr. Cleland's background includes seagoing as a cadet and navigating officer, consulting with an international consulting group, full professor and head of departments of accounting and business studies at three universities, chairman of private and public companies, member of the United Nations Small Business Development Committee on South East Asia, and co-founder of the International Christian Chambers of Commerce.

For the past 25 years, he has actively consulted with the accounting profession and their business clients, helping identify and provide solutions for underlying business problems, which led to the crystallization of the concepts underlying Contribution-Based Activity. These concepts have been adopted in varying degree by numerous businesses small and large, with turnovers ranging from $250,000 to over $12 billion.

Learn more at www.tariinfo.com

Acknowledgments

A grain of sand can achieve little or nothing by itself, but in conjunction with many other grains it can be used to build dams, erect houses, and construct highways; so it is with ideas. Without the active support of members of the accounting profession concerned about doing more for their clients, the concepts underlying CBA and TARI, described in this book, would have remained just an idea.

I acknowledge in particular:

The original group of 17 who came together at St John's College, University of Queensland, and who opened up their practices to permit access to their clients.

My computer partner, Trevor Watters, a member of that original group and an accountant turned software guru, whose unique skills made the development of software available, initially for the accounting profession and subsequently for the business end user.

David Hartley, developer of the world's first professional accounting system, who made it possible for me to address those accountants from which the original group was selected and who has continued to provide valuable assistance over the years.

Several hundred partners of accounting practices worldwide who willingly gave time and energy to actively introduce the concepts to their client base.

Owners and managers of businesses, small and large, who have participated and enjoyed the benefits firsthand.

And not least, I want to acknowledge Jeff Olson, editor, whose sharp eye and mature empathy for the subject matter has been instrumental in shaping the contents for layperson as well as professional; Rita Fernando, coordinating editor, whose cheerful support guided the process; and James Fraleigh, copy editor, whose eye for detail is beyond remarkable! Thank you Jeff, thank you Rita, thank you James, and thanks to members of the team standing behind you. Please know you are all truly appreciated.

On behalf of myself and the unnumbered businesses that will find new strength, direction, and purpose from applying the concepts contained in this book, I salute you all.

Introduction

"Contribution Metrics" evolved from a consulting outreach to a printing business experiencing problems. As a professor of management accounting with a consulting background, I thought it would provide an excellent case study for third-year students. The successful outcome, the extent of which surprised both the business owner and myself, led to a new and startlingly simple way of improving profitability.

Recognizing the benefits of this new concept, which over time became known as Contribution-Based Activity (CBA), accounting practices attended my short courses and conducted client-seminars and client workshops to get the message across. Clients ranged from sole proprietorships to multinationals, and size made little difference to the outcomes.

"I can see that I am really in the business of selling time, and product happens to be the output," exclaimed one proprietor following a pricing review of his product range. He was right. The review showed that although he paid for 20,000 hours of potential activity, only 10,000 hours or 50% could be traced to output. Quite clearly, the leakage was adversely affecting the bottom line.

Lying at the core of any business, small or large, retail or nonretail, units of time-related output are inextricably linked to the financial outcome. Yet financial statements make no reference to units of output such as the number of billed production hours in manufacturing, or the number of sales in retail, or the meals (covers) in a restaurant, and so forth.

As this book goes to print, there is still no seamless connection between a sale and its related units of activity as recorded in financial accounts. As a result, while some decision-makers may be confident of a profit when pricing or quoting a job or a product, comparatively few will know the cumulative extent of gaps between jobs or the resulting impact on their bottom line.

It is extraordinary to realize that despite the latest available software technology, few businesses can seamlessly compare output with input to identify their level of productivity without time-consuming analysis. And as we all know, what isn't known is unlikely to be improved.

The dynamic change that boosted the bottom line in the printing business flowed from linking the gross profit contribution of a sale to the relevant units of activity and tracking the cumulative results against target. Simple though the concept was and still is, my experience over the ensuing years has shown that its very simplicity can inhibit comprehension and obscure the dynamism of its impact. In particular, for those who specialize in financial and management accounting, the concept invariably needs time to sink in.

One public accountant in particular comes to mind. He arranged a seminar at which I addressed about 100 of his clients. This was followed by a several days of interviews to get his clients up and running with CBA. Two years later, he suddenly appeared out of the blue shouting, "I've got it, damn it, I've got it!"

This book has been written in the hope that businesses everywhere will "get it" and in doing so relieve a sizable chunk of the stress on owners, management, and staff that presses unceasingly from all sides.

CHAPTER 1

Background to Contribution-Based Activity (CBA)

CBA grew out of the need for business to keep the forest in view while working "flat-out" down in the trees.

The accounting section of ABCo finalizes an $8,000 invoice for Job 143. Because the job has taken longer than expected, management discounts the bill 5% before sending an invoice for $7,600 to the customer.

Unknown to management, which considers the business to be running "flat-out," productivity is running at the rate of 15,000 billable hours and not the planned 20,000 hours required to achieve the output upon which so much depends. The business is heading for a shortfall of $250,000.

Chapter 1 | Background to Contribution-Based Activity (CBA)

That ignorance of such key positional information can come about in a company equipped with the latest commercial software and professionally qualified personnel is the story underlying the struggle for survival and growth that pervades all categories of business, whether it be manufacturing, service, retail, hospitality, transport, and not least, the professions.

My early belief that all a business needed to stay on track was a monthly financial and management report, a cash-flow report, and a few Key Performance Indicators (KPIs) turned out to be the great deception.

It is also the story underlying Contribution-Based Activity.[1]

The Problem

In the decade following the late 1960s, small and medium-sized businesses,[2] known collectively as SMEs, represented over 94% of all businesses and contributed over 50% of the gross domestic product. However, references to SMEs in management literature, which flowed mainly from the United States, were embryonic and sparse.

Academia, attempting to pinpoint the nature and extent of this "new phenomenon," attended national and international conferences, presented papers, made observations, claimed sightings, extrapolated data from voluminous surveys, and hypothesized about perceived needs. Despite opposition from within, a few brave university faculties grudgingly permitted the inclusion of an SME subject or two as part of a business or economics course.

Government interest also gathered momentum, and international missions were established to define the problems and prescribe solutions. Extensive reports revealed that in essence, SMEs wanted cheaper, more readily available finance by way of loan or equity, less union interference and government regulation, and a restriction on monopoly competition.

Accepting the findings as the real rather than perceived needs, and recognizing the importance of the SMEs to the economy, business advisory agencies were established to address the needs of this sector.

Textbooks on SMEs filtered into the marketplace covering the same functional areas of business that applied to large corporations, such as marketing, production, personnel, and finance, the essential difference being they were slimmer publications. The needs of SMEs were considered to be the same as big business, but smaller.

---

[1]Contribution-Based Activity (CBA) has application for all segments of industry and commerce, including manufacturing, service, professions, wholesale/retail, hospitality, transport, construction, and primary industry.
[2]Reference to small and medium enterprises is not intended to exclude large enterprises, which invariably commence as SMEs.

Nowhere was this more the case than with subjects related to accounting, where a sole-proprietor firm employing a staff of five would be advised to establish and monitor costs and prices along precisely the same principles as a multi-staffed, multi-departmentalized, publicly listed corporate firm.

So ingrained was this attitude, that in the early 1980s, those in the accounting profession aware of the existence of SMEs advocated the solution as requiring more profit-and-loss statements to back up the annual statutory return for tax purposes.[3]

Monthly or quarterly profit-and-loss statements, however, were presented in exactly the same format as the annual statement. There were no budget columns against which actual results could be compared; no gross profit or expense percentages against sales, and no useful ratios or KPIs.

As the 1980s progressed, budget columns made their appearance, and in the 1990s certain ratios and other statistical data were added. Little else has changed except the sheer volume of information output, which had multiplied a hundredfold in computer printouts.

Even so, for the cash-driven proprietor of a typical SME, struggling to pay wages, contain the demands of creditors, appease the bank manager, balance the inventory, handle complaints, improve market share, impart direction, and sustain morale at work and at home, the monthly or quarterly profit-and-loss statement went unread into the same drawer as the annual statement.

For accountants, consultants, and others involved at the coalface, shop floor, or office working with SMEs, it became increasingly obvious that there had to be a better way of serving their needs than by simply providing smaller doses of the medicine prescribed for large corporates.

The traditional accounting approach to diagnosis called for an in-depth analysis of historical data as a basis for prescribing improvement or change. Yet the historical data of most SMEs, if available at all, was fragmentary, unreliable, and out of date. There was also the question of costs, coupled with a defensive attitude about using "management advisers" prevalent in all businesses, small or large.[4]

The solution to tackling the needs of SMEs of necessity had to be different from that applicable to their big brothers. Diagnosis of problems would need to flow from data extracted in such a way that the very process of extraction would itself provide insight for proprietor and staff.

---

[3] I confess to being one of the leading advocates of such an approach at the time!
[4] The defensive attitude toward using consultants was largely broken down in the corporates after decades of marketing by the McKinseys of the world, to the point where the first call by CEOs needing to resolve a burdensome problem is now to a consultant.

For those seriously involved in the search for a workable solution, there were many times when it seemed as elusive as the proverbial needle in the haystack.

The Solution

A breakthrough came when the manager of a printing firm asked for help. He couldn't understand why, after he marked up every job by 25% to make a profit, the business never made more than 5% at the end of a year.

He was pricing jobs in line with traditional accounting methodology contained in the Printing and Allied Trades Manual, where all expenses are distributed to "cost centers" according to a well-established procedure.

For example, the cost of printing carried out on, say, the Heidelberg printing press would include a cost to cover the need for future replacement, a cost to cover its share of the rent of the building based on the space allocated for its use, a cost to cover the electric power to run it, and a cost for wages of the printer operating the unit.

These costs were referred to as "direct" costs because they could be traced to the machine itself; they would make up around 40% of the eventual cost for work carried out on the Heidelberg. The remaining 60%, known as "indirect" costs, were added to cover "overhead" costs involved in supervision, marketing, distribution, administration, and finance. Both direct and indirect costs would be allocated in proportion to the planned operating hours of the machine, a process repeated for other cost centers such as compositing, binding, cutting, packaging, and shipping.

A similar methodology with minor variations applied across businesses engaged in manufacturing, trades, and service, where percentages were added to the cost of purchases and wages to cover indirect overheads, plus another percentage to cover profit. Whatever the method, the final outcome theoretically depended on the level of billable activity.[5]

This system of costing and pricing, although correct in theory, failed in practice. Individual jobs, priced in the office, routed into production, and eventually invoiced out, were captured in the financial accounting system as sales and printed out as such in the period profit-and-loss statements. While in theory the production hours underpinning the sales were accumulated in

---

[5]While the focus here is on production-hours, billable units of activity can refer to a production-hour, an invoiced sale, a cash ring-up in retailing, a bed-night in a hotel/motel, a meal in a restaurant (called a *cover* in the industry), a ton/mile in transport, and so forth. Of the numerous activities occurring in business, the billable unit is fundamental to the activity of the rest.

"management accounts," there was—and is—no seamless connection between hours billed and invoiced sales.

Pricing on the basis that 10,000 hours would be billable, when the actual billing was closer to 5,000 hours, meant the business was unknowingly heading for the rocks, unhelped by financial statements arriving two or three weeks into the following period and providing no information about the units of activity billed or planned, upon which pricing was based.

This was the reason the printer ended up with the equivalent of 3 hours of output for every 8-hour day.

As far as the printer was concerned, the noise of one or more printing machines chattering away in the distance, in conjunction with multiple phone calls, questions to be resolved, wages to be paid, cash to be collected, and any number of decisions required, meant the business was flat-out.[6]

At the time of the printer's cry for help, we were unaware of any fast-track approach to determining the level of output, so we put time checks on the machines and found they were operating for less than 3 hours a day, compared with a planned 5.5 hours.

It was at that point I came to realize that what I had been teaching and advocating, in line with an accounting profession of teachers, lecturers, and practitioners, was missing the mark as far as meeting the real and vital decision-making needs of business.

Focusing on how the billable production-hour could be seamlessly connected and tracked with the invoiced sale, I wondered what would happen if we lumped all the annual expenses together, added a target profit, and came up with one total amount that needed to be recovered?

If the total were divided by the planned billable hours, the result would give a target average gross profit contribution per hour, while the cost of purchases, which varied from job to job, would be left out of the equation to be added at the time of invoicing. ("Target average gross profit contribution per hour" became known as "target average rate index" or "TARI®," to emphasize its benchmark status, and its applicability to any type of business.)

---

[6] At the time this book went to print, financial statements made no mention of productivity, nor were they legally required to do so; neither was there any seamless connection between billed units of activity and the invoiced sale in any major commercial software. This is driven largely by the regulatory demands of government bureaucracies interested only in the bottom line for tax purposes, which places pressure on the practicing accountant.

In theory at least, such tracking would provide:

1. A target average contribution per unit (TARI) as a benchmark against which the actual contribution per unit of a quote or a price could be compared and adjusted as required to improve profitability.
2. A means of tracking and comparing total billed units and gross profit contribution with target weekly and accumulatively.
3. An immediate awareness of the impact of either Item 1 or 2 on the bottom line.

Over the ensuing months, the business began to hum with the printer's growing awareness of how to gain a competitive advantage in acquiring new customers. Cash flow improved and profits began to flow.[7]

Thinking we might have freakishly tapped into a one-off vein of gold, I made sure the printer kept up his traditional pricing system—just in case. However, as time passed, it became obvious that it was what the business needed: a clear view of the forest while working flat-out down in the trees.

I eventually called the simple methodology I employed "Contribution-Based Activity" or CBA, occasionally referred to as the flip side of the traditionally oriented Activity-Based Costing,[8] which had taken root in a profession favoring pinpoint accuracy over practical reality.

TARI became the key derivative of CBA. For example, a business with a gross profit of $1 million[9] and an output of 1 million cans of beans has an average gross profit of $1.00 per can. If the business targets a gross profit of $1,200,000 and 1 million cans of beans for the next period, it can be said to have a TARI of $1.20 per can.

The TARI of $1.20 provides a benchmark against which the gross profit per can is measured. Too many cans sold for a gross profit less than $1.20 will adversely impact the bottom line. The key to avoiding that is to track both the number of cans and the average gross profit per can, weekly and accumulatively, for comparison with target.

---

[7]Chapter 3 has more detail about this business.
[8]A methodology now discredited as being too expensively time consuming by its founders, and since replaced with "Time-Based ABC."
[9]Gross profit is the amount left over to cover expenses and profit after deducting the cost of goods or materials purchased. It is referred to as *gross profit, gross profit contribution,* or *contribution* throughout the book. It equates to (sales − cost of goods/materials), or (total overheads ÷ expenses + profit).

With the help of practicing accountants, CBA was applied to an increasing number of businesses across the spectrum of commerce and industry, including wholesale and retail, hospitality and transport, construction, and agriculture.

It became possible to seamlessly connect the underlying units driving activity with the gross profit contribution by means of a sample invoice analysis that teased out the contribution per unit. It was a process of enlightenment that invariably surprised and often shocked management as the range of gross profit contributions became evident.

The same analysis, taken a step further, provided a close approximation of overall productivity, which in turn became instrumental in getting the importance of the message through to the managers of companies small, medium, and large, opening the door to looking ahead and developing a TARI.[10]

Simple though the concept turned out to be, it was not easy for those steeped in the accounting mind-set to accept. How could direct costs be mixed up with indirect costs? How could wages, power, insurance, phones, and the like be so fixed that you could get an average unit rate across the board? How could a markup on the cost of purchases be left out of the equation?

I understood those questions and the traditional teaching that lay behind them. However, practical reality indicated that the attempt to achieve pinpoint accuracy in the distribution of expenses only served to clutter a clear view of the forest. From both the customer and owner's viewpoint, it was the quality of the output in conjunction with the price that mattered, not how it was made up or by whom.

CBA is based on the assumption that all in-house expenses remain "fixed," like the rent, on the understanding that any significant change in expenses will be reflected in adjustments to TARI[11] on a monthly or quarterly basis.

As long as there is consistency in defining "contribution," whatever costing system is in use, comparison of the contribution per unit of activity with TARI in conjunction with the number of billed units remains the key to survival and profitability. The more sophisticated the costing system, the greater the necessity for a clear view of the forest.

Whatever the business, the level of activity can be targeted[12] and broken down into "units" of activity that are then divided into the target contribution.

---

[10] Readers will find several examples of invoice analysis demonstrating a range of contributions per unit and identifying productivity in the ensuing case studies, especially in Chapter 23.

[11] That expenses could in any way be "fixed" like the rent is an anathema to certain members of the accounting profession, who have tended to lead the way in the opposite direction.

[12] Such as "75% or 6 out of 8 available hours" in manufacturing/service sectors, or "XX number of sales" in retail.

There are times when the selected key activity driver doesn't work as well as it should and may need a trial with another activity—for example, a sheep-leather tanning business, where the contribution per skin proved more workable than contribution per man-hour.

As will be demonstrated in Chapter 5, units of activity and contribution can be likened to two levers: a reduction in one can lead to an increase in the other and vice versa.

Finally, it begs the question: "Why don't current financial and management software systems provide this information?" In the case of manufacturing and service companies, current commercial software is not programmed to extract the unit contribution of an invoiced transaction. The reasons for that include:

1. No regulatory requirement for financial statements to refer to unit input or output;[13]
2. Management accounts emphasize unit cost rather than unit contribution;[14]
3. No overt demand to compare "actual" with "target" unit contribution or knowledge of the benefits of doing so.

Given these limitations, important information relating to an improved bottom-line performance is absent from decision making from the time of quoting or pricing through to the point of sale.

Action Sheets

Achieving a clear view of the forest is one thing, but sustaining a clear view is another. My consulting days with an international group had drilled in the need for follow-through, without which the most highly regarded and well-intentioned plans fall down.

The weekly or fortnightly action meeting, with actions needed noted by whom and by when, is a vital tool in the CBA tool kit. Used correctly, an action meeting of no more than an hour in length will cut through the clutter of talk and pinpoint what is to be done. When a matter is raised and uncertainty exists, responsibility for clarification by way of a summary feedback report

---

[13] In other words, no reference to productivity.
[14] For those looking to compare CBA with systems such as Absorption Costing, Marginal Costing, Time-Based, or Activity-Based Costing, the key difference lies in CBA's focus on tracking the individual unit-contribution in conjunction with the target number of unit-contributions required to cover expenses plus profit. Costing systems focus on the accuracy of the unit cost, and assume management will apply a markup percentage to cover profit.

is accepted—usually by the person raising the subject—for presentation at a subsequent meeting.[15]

The key is achieving the agreement of the person who will undertake the action. Failure to carry out the action becomes apparent at the next meeting; there is no recrimination, merely the question, "When will you do it?" and a date noted. The pressure is subtle and highly effective.

Table 1-1 provides a typical example of an action meeting as recorded on an Action Sheet.

Table 1-1. Action Sheet

Item	Action	Who	When
Invoices	Extract the contribution from each invoice weekly and divide by the production hours to identify the contribution	Max and BK	7/10
Tracking results	Track the invoices weekly and accumulatively for comparison with TARI and the target billable hours	Max and BK	7/10
Meetings	Commence weekly meeting with key staff to review previous week's performance and plan week ahead	Max, BK, HG	7/17
Quoting	Compare the contribution per hour of quotes with the TARI benchmark before submitting quote	Max and JK	7/10

Present at meeting: Max, BK, HG, KC

Summary

The following chapters and appendices show how the theory outlined in this chapter works out in the real world. They will answer your questions about Contribution-Based Activity and TARI, and they will show you how to apply the method to your own business. Done right, you will improve your firm's productivity and profitability.

---

[15] See Chapter 22 for a more complete explanation of action meetings.

Here's a rundown of this chapter's important points:

- Sample invoice analysis identifies productivity, establishes a basis for planning ahead, and eliminates the need for time- and expense-consuming analyses of unreliable and fragmentary historical data.
- The process of planning and targeting improved performance leads to the development of a benchmark known as TARI (Target Average Rate Index).
- Comparison of unit contribution with TARI when quoting or pricing provides the opportunity for adjustment up or down prior to commitment.
- Used in conjunction with a knowledge of the bottom line gained by weekly and accumulative feedback, the comparison provides an unique competitive advantage.
- Weekly and accumulative summary of contribution per unit of key activity is a cost-effective means of comparing real-time performance with potential performance.
- A weekly review of results held in an action meeting format underpins and ensures effective follow-through.
- In the words of the financial director of a major consulting group who based his MBA thesis on a wholesale/retail chain with $12 billion in annual turnover.
- "Movement of profitability analysis to the invoice level provides management with on-line tools for benchmarking and productivity control. Combined with an appropriate IT solution, it lets management identify potentially poor as well as outstanding performance prior to the activity occurring."

CHAPTER 2

Kitchen Utensil Manufacturer Taken to the Cleaners

Following the installation of new hardware and software, growing doubts about the viability of the business prompt the CEO to ask for help.

I had just finished speaking to a group of business executives and was packing my computer prior to catching a taxi to the airport when one of the CEOs, Brian, tapped me on the shoulder.

"Would you have time to speak with the accountant at my plant?" he asked.

The time was 11:30 a.m. "I really need to be at the airport by 12:30 to catch the my flight out," I replied with a sympathetic smile.

Chapter 2 | Kitchen Utensil Manufacturer Taken to the Cleaners

"Well, the plant is on the way. If you could just spare 20 minutes, I could get you to the airport in good time." There was such a sense of need in his tone that I agreed to go with him.

On the way, he told me his plant manufactured kitchen utensils for nationwide distribution, and that they had recently upgraded all their information systems with new hardware and software at a cost of $500,000. The upgrades were designed to improve overall control of inventory, production, and pricing.

Although the system was designed and installed by one of the Big Four accounting firms, in whom he had complete trust, the information pouring out was so extensive he felt he had lost his grip on the business. That, in conjunction with a slowing down of cash flow, told him things were not as they should be.

While he was talking, I was trying to focus on what lay ahead.

Experience had taught me various ways of getting to the heart of a business without spending too much time on analysis. In the case of Brian's business, I assumed it would be a matter of either

1. comparing production hours billed with production hours available for billing,[1] or
2. comparing the company's planned average gross profit[2] per production hour with the actual gross profit per hour in sales to one or more major customers.[3]

Either way, given the limited time available, I would have to play it by ear.

At the plant, I was ushered into a conference room where, to my surprise, the accountant sat waiting, together with the consultant responsible for designing and installing the software. To suggest the atmosphere was distinctly chilly would be an understatement.

I went straight to the whiteboard. "Can you give me budgeted sales, materials at cost, and production hours for the year?" I asked the accountant, wondering how long it would take to get the information.

He had no trouble locating the figures and I wrote them on the board (Table 2-1).

---

[1] Table 2-1 makes this clear.
[2] Throughout this book, *gross profit* is defined as the contribution toward covering in-house expenses and profit. It is the amount left over from a sale, after deducting the cost price of materials used. It can be referred to as *gross profit, gross profit contribution,* or *contribution.*
[3] Table 2-2 provides an example.

Table 2-1. Target Average Contribution per Hour

A	Sales	$60,000,000
B	Materials at Cost Price	$40,000,000
C = (A − B)	Gross Profit Contribution[4]	$20,000,000
D	Production Hours	250,000 hours
E = (C ÷ D)	Target Average Contribution per Hour	$80

"That's not how we calculate gross profit," the accountant snapped. "We add factory wages and costs to the materials before deducting from sales."

I understood where he was coming from: it was a traditionally accepted approach to add factory wages and expenses to materials before working out gross profit.

"Well, let's face it," I replied, "the days of hire and fire from job queues have faded, and factory wages and expenses are about as fixed as most other expenses. However, the costs of materials used can and do vary considerably from job to job." The accountant frowned.

I continued, "In any event, what we are looking for here is a benchmark based on the average contribution of all the production hours. It happens to be $80. Depending on the job, the customer, and the sale price, some hours will result in higher contribution, and some lower."

I pressed for a response. "Would you accept the company needs an average gross profit contribution per production hour of $80?" I asked the accountant.

Several seconds passed before he nodded agreement.

"Would you also agree that knowing the planned average of $80 provides a benchmark for comparing the gross profit per hour of a quote or a sale?"

"I guess so," he said, clearly wondering where it was all heading.

I said, "I refer to the $80 benchmark as TARI, short for Target Average Rate Index, to avoid confusing it with a cost or a price. It is probably one of the most important—if not *the* most important—of KPIs."[5]

"Never heard of it!" he said.

"Well, let's see why I say that," I continued. "Who's your biggest customer?"

---

[4] The $20 million gross profit contribution is the total of planned expenses plus profit.
[5] KPI: Key Performance Indicator.

Chapter 2 | Kitchen Utensil Manufacturer Taken to the Cleaners

The accountant mentioned the household name of the country's largest distributer of kitchen utensils.

"How much of your output do they take?" I asked.

The accountant shrugged. "No idea off the top of my head," he said.

"Fifty-five percent," Brian interjected.

"Can we access three or four typical invoices for this customer together with the cost of materials used and production hours involved?" I asked.

"Sure," he said, gesturing to the accountant to comply.

While the accountant left the room to locate the invoices, the consultant broke the silence to drive home his credentials, pointing out that in addition to his role as a senior consultant with one of the Big Four, with extensive involvement with major companies in the region, he lectured on management accounting part time at the university.

The accountant returned. With three invoices in hand, it took less than five minutes to demonstrate the average gross profit per production hour for this customer (Table 2-2).

Table 2-2. Invoice Analysis of Number One Customer

Invoice No.	Invoice Price Net of Tax ($) A	Materials Used ($) B	Gross Profit Contribution ($) C = A − B	Gross Profit (%) D = C ÷ A	# of Hours E	Average $ Per Hour F = C ÷ E
2765	100,000	68,000	32,000	32	914	35
2958	300,000	200,000	100,000	33	3,125	32
3015	150,000	102,000	48,000	32	1,450	33
Total	550,000	370,000	180,000	33	5,489	33

I pointed out, "It seems you are getting an average gross profit contribution of $33 per hour from a customer taking 55% of output when you really need an average of $80!" There was dead silence.

"What does it mean then?" Brian's query had an anxious tone.

"It means your best customer is absorbing 55% of 250,000 production hours," I went back to whiteboard (Table 2-3).

Table 2-3. Implications for Balance of Customers

A	250,000 hours × $80 =	$20,000,000
B	(250,000 × 55%) =	137,500 hours
C	137,500 hours × $33 =	$4,537,500
D = (A – C)	Balance Required =	$15,462,500
E	Hours Available (250,000 hours – 137,500) =	112,500 hours
F = (D ÷ E)	Average Rate per Hour Required =	$137.44

"The bad news is that from the balance of the 112,500 hours in the year, you will need to achieve a total contribution of $15,462,500—at an average of $137+ per hour—if you are going to achieve your planned gross profit contribution of $20 million."

Brian looked shell-shocked. "What do you suggest, then?" he queried, grasping for a ray of light.

"Well, any reduction in the number of production hours scheduled for your best customer would help ease the burden. It's a matter of thinking outside the box about ways and means of improving efficiency in production to get the hours down. A reduction of 10% in the 137,500 hours currently absorbed by your best customer would make additional hours available for other customers and help reduce the required hourly contribution."

I continued, "You can also look at ways and means of reducing material costs through buying better and cutting back on waste. A 5% reduction in the $40 million material costs would improve the overall contribution by $2 million; 10% would be better!"

I told the group I would carry out a sample invoice analysis on the other 45% of customers to see what they were getting by way of contribution. I knew they would be surprised![6]

"I really think it's time to get going to the airport," I said, placing the whiteboard marker back in its slot.

Reaching for his car keys on the table, Brian gave a loud sigh. "I knew I was being screwed," he said, "I just didn't know how much!"

As we left the room, the eyes of both the accountant and the consultant were fixed on the whiteboard, struggling to come to terms with the findings.

---

[6]An invoice analysis similar to that carried out on the number one customer could also be carried out on a representative sample of the remaining 45% of customers to assess the range of gross profit contributions per hour.

As we drove off, Brian said, "They threatened to take their business offshore if we didn't lower our prices," said Brian, referring to his best customer. "I knew something was wrong but couldn't put my finger on it. Guess I allowed myself to be persuaded by all the calculations the accountant came up with about the deal making a marginal contribution."

Case Comment

I leaned back in my seat as the flight took off, thinking of Brian and the half-million he had spent installing hardware and software to get control of his business, only to find he was unable to see the forest for the trees. More to the point, the installation had failed to provide the key information that he needed when making decisions vital to the future viability of the company.

I wondered why it should be so difficult to identify that the best customer is contributing $33 an hour compared with a, TARI of $80.

The fact is, whatever the category of business, be it manufacturing or retailing, trucking or construction, most businesses do not analyze invoices to highlight gross profit per unit[7] along the lines demonstrated in Table 2-2.

What's more, a cornerstone of the accounting profession proclaims the need for information to be timely and relevant. In Brian's situation, as with 95% of businesses, the feedback was neither timely nor relevant.

Such feedback is not relevant when it fails to indicate the level of productivity,[8] nor is it timely when it arrives two or three weeks into the following month. A problem that could have been resolved at the outset can become increasingly difficult to remedy some weeks later. Thus the need for weekly feedback.[9]

The following real-life case history of a printing business highlights the problem of identifying the levels of output activity—normally referred to as productivity. The case happens to be the printer who sparked my original involvement with the CBA concepts underlying TARI.

---

[7] A unit of activity is an hour in manufacturing, an invoiced sale, a cash ring-up in wholesale/retail, a "cover" in restaurants/cafes, a minute in the rag trade, and so forth.
[8] Financial statements such as the profit and loss and balance sheet make no mention of productivity.
[9] See Table 1-2 for a useful weekly and accumulative tracking format. Following traditional accounting methodology, commercial software is not programmed to seamlessly connect production hours in the job ledger with relevant data in the financial accounts and is normally geared to providing monthly feedback.

CHAPTER 3

Printing Business Multiplies Net Profit by 500%

Unable to see a connection between adding 25% profit to every job and ending up with 5%, the printer is instrumental in giving birth to TARI

"I don't understand it at all: I put 25 percent profit on every job and never get more than 5 percent by the end of the year. What am I doing wrong?" asked the printer.

"I don't know," I replied, "but we can soon find out." After 12 years as a professor of accounting and business studies, specializing in management accounting, I had yet to learn how to pinpoint the cause of such problems without extensive, time-consuming analysis. Nevertheless, I was confident we would find the solution.

Chapter 3 | Printing Business Multiplies Net Profit by 500%

Seeing the exercise as a potential hands-on challenge for final-year students, I sent three of them to the printing firm to collect a sample of jobs for analysis. When they came back with 3,000 job envelopes selected at random from the previous three years, I was not entirely unhappy to note the task would last for several tutorials.

Eventually the analysis was completed. "Just as he said, he puts an average of 25 percent profit on every job," they reported, "and ends up with 5 percent."

"So what's the conclusion?" I asked.

"Well, he's right!" they answered with a smile.

I mentally questioned the value of three years of conventional accounting studies.

Sensing the problem was connected with too many gaps between jobs, and lacking any other information, we decided to check the length of time each printing machine operated. Gaining the cooperation of very skeptical employees, we ran the check for five days, only to find the six printing machines operated for less than two hours each out of an eight-hour day.

In the face of the printer's refusal to accept the findings, we ran the check for another week with much the same result.

While the time check was underway, I spent time observing the routine. It went something like this: a customer would ask for 10,000 letterheads "the same as last time." The work envelope for the previous occasion was located and a new job card inserted. The foreman looked at the job and wrote down the estimated times for compositing, printing, guillotining, and binding.

The job card was forwarded in the envelope to the person graced with the title of cost accountant. He in turn reached for a plastic-covered A4 sheet containing the costs for every category of work. Taking account of the foreman's times, he jotted down the costs on the job card in pencil.

At the completion of the job, the owner took the job envelope home along with 30 or so other envelopes in order to finalize the pricing over a weekend. This process involved reviewing the proposed prices on the job card, then adjusting them as he considered would be in line with previous billings, adding to—or subtracting from—the prices according to his best knowledge of the client and his "feelings" for an appropriate fit.

I recall being mildly shocked to realize that the exact, if not exacting, science[1] of cost accounting, which occupies a significant portion of an undergraduate degree, had but passing relevance to the realities of pricing in practice.

---

[1] "Art" may be more apt.

The Printing and Allied Trades Manual for association members set out the complete rationale of costing and pricing precisely as would be found in any management accounting textbook. Nevertheless, having established various costs according to accepted theory, the owner's interest appeared to terminate at that point. Each job was seen to be contributing to profit, but in absence of the company's tracking the accumulated total of all jobs completed and billed, the theory broke down. Monthly financial statements, appearing weeks after the events to which their contents referred, did not refer to gaps between jobs or identify productivity by comparing hours billed with hours available for billing.

Driven to find cash to meet the weekly wage bill and satisfy demanding suppliers as well as an anxious bank manager, the owner's prime target was cash, not profit, for as far as he was concerned, the two were identical. Cash in the bank meant wages and anxious suppliers could be paid without too much stress.

"As I see it," I said to him, following several weeks of reviewing the whole process of theory and practice, "excluding paper, ink, negatives, and outsourced work, you need to cover $350,000 in expenses for the year. If you add a further $100,000 to cover net profit, you need a gross profit contribution of $450,000."

In view of a record profit of $35,000 achieved five years earlier, his look of disbelief at the $100,000 profit was palpable.

I pressed on. "You have 10 staff engaged in hands-on production with 1,800 hours each available for billing, or 18,000 hours in total. Assuming 50% of those hours can be charged to jobs—bearing in mind last year was a lot less according to the checks we made—then you have 9,000 hours to achieve $450,000, or an average of $50 contribution[2] per hour."

He threw up his hands. "Our hourly charge rates are $20. We'd go out of business in a month."

I picked up an invoice for $900 lying on his desk. "What was the cost of materials used in this job?" I asked.

He seemed to know the answer without referring to the work envelope. "Three hundred dollars," he said.

"How many hours did you estimate the job would take when you quoted?"

"Ten hours."

---

[2]*Contribution* refers to what is commonly referred to as gross profit contribution, being the amount left over after deducting the cost of goods or materials used; it "contributes" to covering overhead expenses plus any net profit. In other words, contribution = (overheads + net profit). Alternatively, contribution = (sales – cost of goods or materials); or net profit = (contribution – overheads).

I deducted $300 from the $900 and divided the remaining $600 contribution by 10 hours.

"Well," I said, "that works out at $60 an hour." I showed him the figures appearing in Table 3-1.

Table 3-1. Identifying Average Contribution per Hour

A	Invoice Sale Price	$900
B	Materials at Cost	$300
C = (A − B)	Contribution	$600
D	Units Billed[3]	10 hours
E = (C ÷ D)	Average Unit Contribution	$60

He stared in disbelief. "How come?" he asked.

"Well, you applied a markup percentage to materials followed by a markup percentage to labor to cover overheads and a further 25% to cover profit, plus a little extra to cover your 'feelings.' All of which brings a contribution toward covering expenses and profit of $60 an hour."

"But that includes profit and markup and everything," he observed.

"That's right, and that's what the overall target average contribution rate of $50 includes.[4] The key is to make sure that in addition to the average of $50 per hour, you bill the target chargeable hours of 9,000 a year, or an average of 200 hours a week for a 45-week year."[5]

He shook his head slowly, intrigued yet mystified.

"Let's run it alongside the existing system for a month or two," I suggested. "We can't go too far off track."

I was even more tentative than the printer, wondering if my efforts at simplification had missed something important. The idea of running it as a trial appealed to me as much as to him.

---

[3]*Unit* refers to the key activity fundamental to output—in this case a production-hour.
[4]To emphasize its benchmark status and avoid confusion with a "cost," the target average contribution rate is known as the Target Average Rate Index or TARI.
[5]52 weeks less 7 weeks (4 weeks annual holiday + 10 days public holidays + 5 days sick leave).

We met every week and checked progress by simply listing billings for the week, deducting the materials from the sale price, and dividing by the quoted or estimated hours. If the contribution of a quote came in at less than $50, he would review ways and means to do the job in less time in order to get closer to or exceed $50.

Billings were tracked weekly and accumulatively to compare hours and contribution with the average weekly target of 200 hours × $50.

As his confidence increased, he began to target jobs showing a higher contribution than $50, as well as fine-tuning the hours of jobs with lower contribution.

It was this step-by-step, quote-by-quote, job-by-job decision making at the shop that began to make the difference.

After 10 weeks, the hours charged to jobs totaled 1,800 hours, or 200 hours below target, but the contribution rate was averaging $60 an hour, or $10 above the $50 benchmark. The business was running $8,000 ahead of targeted net profit. Table 3-2 illustrates a simple format for tracking weekly results for comparison with target.

Table 3-2. Monitoring Results: 10-Week Comparison with Target

	Total Weeks A	Total Hours B	Average Contribution C	Total Contribution D = (B × C)
Target	10 Weeks	2,000 Hours	$50 (TARI)	$100,000
Actual	10 Weeks	1,800 Hours	$60	$108,000
Variance		–200 Hours	+$10	+$8,000

Encouraged, we pressed on, and after 20 weeks found that 3,600 billed hours were 400 hours below target, but the average hourly rate had escalated to $65, or $15 above target. In all, the firm was $34,000 ahead of targeted net profit (Table 3-3).

Table 3-3. Monitoring Results: 20-Week Comparison with Target

	Total Weeks A	Total Hours B	Average Contribution C	Total Contribution D = (B × C)
Target	20 Weeks	4,000 Hours	$50 (TARI)	$200,000
Actual	20 Weeks	3,600 Hours	$65	$234,000
Variance		–400 Hours	+$15	+$34,000

Being well ahead of target, we discussed the possibility of getting a foot in the door of one or two larger companies in order to quote for long-run jobs that could keep the machines running in the down times.

With his growing awareness of where the bottom line was located, the owner was in a position to underquote any competitor if he wished and still make a contribution to the bottom line, providing he left some margin on materials.

Keen to follow up on getting long-run orders that could be tackled over a period of weeks, he asked me if I would join him in visiting a major mining group to see if he could secure an initial order. As he offered to pay the airfare, I agreed to go with him.

It proved to be an interesting experience. After querying the whereabouts of the printing company's regional location, the purchasing manager politely indicated that all printing requirements were met out of two major cities.

Noting the disconsolate look on the printer's face, I spoke up. "It would be great if you could manage a small order. It's just that we have students looking at the costing structure of this printing firm, and they believe they have worked out a new way of pricing that really works and would like to try it out on a large company. You will no doubt save money."

He looked at me for a long time before saying, "Well, you've come a long way. I'll see what we can do."

Digging into a pile of files, he pulled out a purchase requisition for an interim report to shareholders. "Can you give a quote on 50,000?"

The printer flicked through the report and asked for a calculator.

"I don't expect a quote here and now," said the purchasing manager. "Take it away with you, and let me have a price next week!"

"I can give a price now if you wish," said the owner.

"No—take it away and let me have it next week." It was obvious he had no desire to take advantage of what was in his eyes a small-time printing firm in a country location he had never heard of.

The printer forwarded a quote within two days and received an order by the end of the week. In time, he went on to secure long-term contracts from the three major mining companies in the state.

Following his election as state president of the Printing and Allied Trades Association, he was nominated to chair the National Conference for Printers. I suggested it might be a good idea to prepare a joint paper for presentation to the participants on what had obviously proved to be a significant breakthrough.

"Great idea," he said, "I did think about asking you to speak, but on second thought decided it could wait until the next national conference."

"Any particular reason?" I asked.

"Well, I'll be retired by then!" he said with a big smile.

Some years later, after taking up a new position in another city about four hours' drive from the printer, I received a call from the proprietor of the local newspaper, asking if we could meet. When I asked him what he had in mind, he said, "Do I understand correctly that you were instrumental in helping XYZ printing firm with their pricing system some time ago?"

I replied in the affirmative.

"Well," he said, "I was wondering if you could do the same for us. It's just that XYZ is down here taking a lot of our business."

Case Comment

Some years later, I was consulting with an accounting practice that had been attempting to improve the performance of one of their clients, which operated a medium-sized printing firm.

The accounting firm had been working with the printer to develop an improved costing system. After six months of analyzing past performance and calculating costs at various productivity levels across 10 cost centers, they had accumulated a mass of data but were at a loss to see the way forward.

Listening to my story of the printer who had done so well, the owner of this printing firm, which had a $12 million turnover, wondered what relevance the story had for his much larger business.

I explained that just as the principle of gravity applies regardless of size, so it is with the concept of contribution-based activity that underlies TARI. It is universally applicable regardless of size.

Like the printer, a business may have planned for a certain level of sales and profit, but only finds out along the way, usually as cash flow falters, that the plan has fallen by the wayside.

The case history of the printer highlights a key problem facing business in general, retail and nonretail, large and small: chasing sales based on the traditional approach to pricing jobs or products while overlooking the basis upon which pricing is established—the level of billable output.

For example, if a target contribution covering expenses and profit of $450,000 is allocated to a planned 15,000 units of output activity which fades over time to 9,000 units, then the required contribution will rise from $30 to $50 per unit (Tables 3-4a and 3-4b).

Table 3-4a. Contribution Rate Based on 15,000 Hours

A	Target Contribution	$450,000
B	Target Unit Output	15,000 Hours
C = (A ÷ B)	Target Average Rate	$30 per Hour

Table 3-4b. Contribution Rate Based on 9,000 Hours

A	Target Contribution	$450,000
B	Target Unit Output	9,000 Hours
C = (A ÷ B)	Target Average Rate	$50 per Hour

Obviously, pricing on the basis of 15,000 units, when you're only doing 9,000, would be heading for trouble.

In summary, of the numerous activities taking place at any one time, there is one key unit of activity fundamental to and driving the rest. In the case of the printer, the key unit is a billable production-hour.

So for the printer, dividing the overall target contribution by the target billable number of units results in a target average unit contribution, referred to as a Target Average Rate Index or TARI. The word *Index* is used to emphasize its statistical or benchmark status to distinguish it from a cost or price.

No matter the company, once TARI is established, the business is in a position to do the following:

1. Compare each quote, job, or sale (in the case of retail) with a benchmark that reflects the aim of the business to achieve a particular profit.

2. Track progress weekly and accumulatively by comparing actual billings with targeted billings as in Table 3-3.

If the real-time level of billings for the business—calculated by comparing actual with target billings for the period to date—is not considered on a week-by-week basis, the connection between billings and the targeted bottom line will remain in limbo. It is possible to catch up on a bad week, but not on a bad month, especially if the feedback arrives two or three weeks into the following month. Normally, weekly and accumulative feedback will be enough to sustain the connection.

TARI can be used to advantage in several ways, one of which will be explored in the following case history.

CHAPTER 4

Furniture Manufacturer Climbs Out of the Red

Six months of fine-tuning by a leading consulting group failed to stem the slide, despite a new product sending the plant into overdrive.

While in the UK, I contacted an old friend, Peter, who was working as a senior consultant with a widely respected international consulting group. He was at that time applying his skills to a major furniture manufacturer on the outskirts of London.

He said he had been on the assignment for the past six months, focusing on improving throughput in the factory and achieving a measure of success. Output was on track and the plant was working overtime to keep up with orders.

Chapter 4 | Furniture Manufacturer Climbs Out of the Red

He had recently turned his attention to streamlining marketing procedures, getting the sales representatives to reassess the value of their calls, and looking at ways and means of establishing a more effective promotional campaign.

Even so, he admitted he had been unable to stem the downward slide in the bottom line.

Knowing he had a grasp of the concepts of CBA and the TARI benchmark, I queried whether he was using them on the assignment. He said that his client employed over 750 people, of whom 26 were in the accounting office and 32 in IT, all highly qualified and providing up-to-date feedback from state-of-the-art software. Given the exponential changes that had taken place in production due to robotic machinery, he considered production-hours of minimal consequence in matters of costing and pricing, and that TARI appeared to him to be focused on production-hours as the key activity driver.

I reminded him that the key production activity in any business, large or small, could vary from business to business and department to department within a business and may be person-hours or robot-hours.[1]

For the sake of friendship, if nothing else, he agreed to carry out a preliminary product analysis along CBA lines, but without mentioning it to his client at the risk of losing face.

As it turned out, despite the extensive use of robotic equipment for cutting, turning, and finishing, the costing was clearly based on production-hours as the common denominator.

It was a simple matter to divide the overall planned gross profit contribution by the planned production-hours to arrive at a TARI of £57 (Table 4-1).

Table 4-1. Identifying TARI

A	Sales	£74,920,000
B	Materials at Cost	£ 43,000,000
C = (A − B)	Gross Profit Contribution[2]	£31,920,000
D	Billable Hours	560,000 man-hours (70% of available hours)
E = (C ÷ D)	TARI	£57

---

[1] Or square meters of partitioning, cans of beans, number of sales measured by cash register checkout or invoice in retailing, meals served in a restaurant, bed-nights in a hospital, room-nights in a motel, and so forth.

[2] Normally referred to as gross profit contribution, unless specified otherwise, the term is used throughout this book to covers total expenses and profit, inclusive of all wages and overheads. It is the amount left after deducting the cost of material purchases.

From there it became a matter of comparing the actual contribution per hour of each of the 120 products with the TARI of £57.

However, because the existing software was programmed to provide feedback in a standard management-accounts format that combined material costs with factory costs such as wages and overheads, the comparison could not be made.

It took Peter a day to explain to the finance director why he wanted to extract the contribution per production-hour per product, and a further day to get the IT manager to understand why the project should be given priority.

Once underway, it took a further three days for a system analyst and two programmers to pinpoint the gross profit contribution per production-hour of each of the 120 products.

"I must say what surprises me is the range of contributions per production-hour," Peter explained when we finally sat down at my sister's home in London to review the results. "I would have expected a much greater consistency than is shown here," he said pointing to contributions ranging from £96 to £22 (Table 4-2).

Table 4-2. Identifying Average Rate per Production-Hour[3]

Product	Sale Price of One Suite (£)	Materials (£)	Contribution	%	Units (Hours)	Average per Unit (£)
Suite 154	3,760	2,518	1,242	33	13	96
Suite 136	2,979	1,956	1,023	34	20	51
Suite 112	3,904	2,655	1,249	32	25	50
Suite 098	2,988	2,002	986	33	19	52
Suite 073	2,490	1,693	797	32	17	47
Suite 055	1,934	1,296	638	33	11	58
Suite 032	2,768	1,910	858	31	24	36
Suite 019	1,374	921	453	33	21	22

---

[3] A sample extracted from the list of 120 products identifies the average contribution rate per hour per suite. The hourly rate would have been calculated on the basis of manufacturing multiple numbers of the suite.

"I assumed the 50% markup on factory cost to cover overheads and profit would have resulted in a more even pattern of hourly rates," he said, "yet only 19 of the 120 products contributed more than £57 per man-hour, and of the 19, at least 4 are discontinued lines," pointing to a discontinued product contributing £96.

It was then his eyes settled on a product contributing £36 per hour.

"Goodness!" he exclaimed. "This is the product they are all excited about. It's selling into Europe like hotcakes and pushing production into overtime!"

He jumped up from his chair. "There's obviously been an error in pricing and it hasn't been picked up!"

"What are you going to do about it?" I asked.

"Take it in and let them see it," he replied, stuffing the papers in his briefcase in a hurried exit to his car.

When we spoke a week or so later, I asked about his progress.

He said, "The finance director wants to start tracking results using the TARI benchmark. He was a bit defensive at first, but I think once he realized it would be better tackled sooner than later, he was happy to get on with it. Interestingly enough, he said he had something similar in mind a year ago but didn't follow through!"

"And the managing director?" I asked.

"A bit early yet. He needs time to let it sink in. He leaves all the figuring to the financial director. Right now, we are checking the gross profit contribution to flow from the products planned for next year."

Another week passed before we met again to discuss progress.

"It would have been a disaster to have continued the way we were going," Peter said. "As I mentioned, we had planned sales by multiplying out the sale price of each product by the number we estimated we would sell and merely applied the estimated gross profit margin based on our 50% markup to arrive at the gross profit contribution. When we reworked the exercise using the TARI approach, the margin worked out far less than our estimates." He showed me an example (Table 4-3).

Table 4-3. Checking the Markup Approach with TARI

A	Target Number of Sales, Suite 098	1,000
B	Factory Cost per Suite	£2,000
C	Total Factory Cost	£2,000,000
D = (50% of C)	Gross Profit Contribution	£1,000,000
E = (C + D)	Total Sales	£3,000,000
F	Units per Suite	23 hours
G = (F × A)	Total Units[4]	23,000 hours
H = (D ÷ G)	Average Contribution per Unit	£43.48
I	TARI	£57.00

It took the managing director two weeks or so to grasp the concept. He had started work with the company as a boy of 14 and worked his way up through production. Now close to retirement age, he found himself confronting a situation that challenged his comprehension: how could a finance department staffed with 26 accountants, several of them professionally qualified, and 32 systems analysts and programmers, all graduates with some postgraduates, have gotten it so wrong?

Calling the department heads together, he got Peter to explain why the company had been experiencing a downward trend in profitability and what was needed to reverse it. This was followed by a brainstorming session focused on improving method and efficiency to reduce production times and determine ways and means of cutting material costs.

Starting with the suite currently in demand and requiring overtime in production, they worked their way through the top-selling suites contributing less than £57, being careful to avoid any change in basic design or quality of appearance.

Over a three-week period, the sessions proved to be effective in gaining additional contribution per production-hour across 25 of the top-selling products, with the contribution from the best-selling product rising from £36 to £48 initially, and eventually, with more fine-tuning, to £56 (Tables 4-4a and 4-4b).

---

[4] A unit of key activity, in this case a production-hour.

Table 4-4a. Selected Product Unit-Contribution Before Change

Product	Sale Price of One Suite (£)	Materials (£)	Contribution (£)	%	Units (Hours)	Average per Unit (£)
Suite 073	2,490	1,693	797	32	17	47
Suite 055	1,934	1,296	638	33	11	58
Suite 032	2,768	1,910	858	31	24	36
Suite 019	1,374	921	453	33	21	22

Table 4-4b. Selected Product Unit-Contribution After Change

Product	Sale Price of One Suite (£)	Materials (£)	Contribution (£)	%	Units (Hours)	Average per Unit (£)
Suite 073	2,490	1,608	882	35	15	59
Suite 055	1,934	1,236	698	36	10	70
Suite 032	2,768	1,760	1,008	36	18	56
Suite 019	1,374	825	549	40	16	34

The accounts department commenced tracking production-hours and unit-contributions of invoiced products singly and accumulatively against target. Within three months, improvements in unit-contributions began to show up with the first sign of an upward trend in the bottom line.[5]

Knowing he needed an average unit-contribution of $57, the managing director lost no time in applying the concept to the design section of the marketing department. New furniture designs calling for his approval were now reviewed in light of their proposed unit-contribution. Any that delivered a contribution of less than £57 were sent back for redesign.[6]

With results proving to be so positive, the managing director considered that he finally had a grip on the business. So much so, that after walking around the factory one Friday afternoon and noting the hours the employees used to clean up before going home—an event that had gone on for as many years as he could recall—he went back to his office and multiplied the hours by £57.

Peter told me he found him with head in hands late that Friday evening, having discovered the cleanup process was depleting the bottom line to the tune of £2 million a year.

---

[5] Table 1-2 illustrates a simple format for tracking weekly results for comparison with target.
[6] This process could hide inefficiencies elsewhere were it not for an ongoing weekly and cumulative tracking process comparing actual with target, underpinning, and sustaining moves for improvement on all fronts.

In the belief that in-house labor was cheaper than outsourcing, he had consistently turned down offers by contractors to do all the cleaning for less than £150,000. However, his previous calculation of in-house versus outsourcing costs was based on an in-house cost of £12 an hour, not the potential £57 that was dependent on the input of that hour.

Before I left the UK, some months later, the bottom line was showing a definite upward trend into profit. Peter was asked to extend his assignment for a further six months.

Case Comment

One can only feel for the managing director in such a situation, surrounded as he was by professionally well-qualified finance and IT departments, including an financial director upon whom he relied completely. His background and focus from the time he started with the business as a boy of 14 had been production. It is not surprising that it took him several days to understand the essence of the matter, only to realize that both the diagnosis and the prescription for resolving the problem were so simple.

It was not as though he lacked information about the business. Along with all directors, he received a 125-page monthly "board pack" covering every aspect of the business, including a detailed list of where performance varied from target. If anything, he suffered from information overload.

Awareness of the direct relationship between the target gross profit and the production-hour gave him a grip on the business that he had never previously enjoyed.

Whereas the printer in the Chapter 3 was unaware that he was getting close to two hours' output for eight hours' pay, in this case, the output was known to be close to 75%, or six hours per eight-hour day.

Even so, no connection had been made between the actual gross profit contribution of a product and its overall targeted contribution.

Assuming the costing had been carried out in line with the costing of all products, how could it happen that a product so much in demand returned such a low contribution per production-hour unit of input?

It could be the time to make and assemble had been miscalculated, or the price of materials had risen without being noticed, reducing the desired margin available.

It could also mean that retailer resistance or competition in the marketplace had caused a price cut or involved discounting.

Chapter 4 | Furniture Manufacturer Climbs Out of the Red

The point is that none of these possibilities were detected in the midst of numerous activities taking place at the same time, and it was only the fortuitous intervention of my meeting up with Peter[7] that restored focus to what really mattered.

The following case study illustrates the interaction between output activity and the contribution per unit of that activity.

---

[7] At the conclusion of his consulting assignment, Peter stayed on as a head of operations, reporting directly to the managing director for another two years or so, before he was headhunted by a pipe-manufacturing group with plants in the US and UK. In March 2013, I had the pleasure of visiting the UK plant and speaking with key personnel. CBA and TARI concepts were clearly in evidence throughout the plant. From the plant manager to the apprentice sweeping the floors, all were aware of the value of their contribution to the bottom line. The employees in each section engaged with different operations, met weekly for an hour to review results for the past week, and established targets for the week ahead. In a plant that worked around the clock in three shifts, the need for supervision was minimal. It was an uplifting experience!

CHAPTER 5

Contractor Overcomes Competition to Make a Profit

Quoting at a price to cover expenses and profit, a contractor finds he cannot win jobs and thinks he must reduce his price. However, doing so would mean forgoing profit

The contractor was 1 of 10 people I nominated for an interview following a seminar at which I had spoken on "How to Detect and Eradicate Malignant Cancer in Your Business." He was intrigued at the thought of week-by-week tracking of billed time and wanted to discuss it further.

Chapter 5 | Contractor Overcomes Competition to Make a Profit

As an electrical contractor, he employed 20 technicians installing electrical circuits in high-rise buildings and had struggled to make a profit during the past year.

Following a brief review of his situation, in conjunction with his accounting adviser, we projected a target contribution by adding the anticipated expenses of the business to a healthy net profit for the year ahead and dividing the result by an estimated number of billable hours.[1] We arrived at a target average contribution[2] per hour of $46 (Table 5-1).

Table 5-1. Target Average Rate Index (TARI)[3]

A	Target Expenses	$1,042,000
B	Target Profit	$200,000
C = (A + B)	Target Contribution	$1,242,000
D	Target Units (Hours)[4]	27,000
E = (C ÷ D)	Target Average (TARI)	$46

He understood that in order to achieve the planned contribution for the year, he would need to track an average of 600 hours a week (20 technicians × 30 hours each) for 45 weeks at an average contribution of $46 an hour.

We completed an Action Sheet (Table 5-2). It set out the key points, and it noted the start dates and the persons responsible.[5]

Table 5-2. Action Sheet

Item	Action	Who	When
Tracking Results	Set up software to track billings for comparison with target of an average 600 billable hours, weekly and accumulatively	NJ	10/5
Review	E-mail copy of set-up to Adviser	NJ	10/5
Next Meeting		AS, HG	10/19

Present at meeting: **AS, HG, KC**

---

[1] Based on charging out 6 hours a day, 5 days a week, and 45 weeks of the year.
[2] *Contribution*, invariably labeled "gross profit contribution," refers to the amount left over after deducting the cost of materials payable to a supplier.
[3] When used as a benchmark, the target average contribution is referred to as the target average rate index, or TARI, to avoid confusion with a cost or a price.
[4] 20 technicians × 30 hours a week × 45 weeks.
[5] Bearing in mind that "genius is 20%, implementation 80%," Chapter 22 contains examples of the vital role of Action Sheets when implementing change.

Pleased with the projected profit and simplified approach to tracking, the contractor was smiling as he left the accountant's office.

It was six months before I had an opportunity to respond to the accountant's request for a follow-up interview. It seems the contractor was not achieving his target and was deeply concerned about where to go and what to do.

"It's too competitive," he said. "I can't win quotes at $46 an hour and my order book is down to three weeks' work at most."

"At what rate can you win quotes?" I asked

"No more than $40," he replied.

Standing with my back to the whiteboard, I looked at him intently. To drop his TARI from $46 to $40 would negate most if not all of his profit.

I mentally reviewed the two levers within our reach:

1. Billable units of activity
2. TARI of $46 per hour

If the TARI of $46 couldn't be achieved, billed output or productivity had to be increased.

However, the tracking data indicated that target billable hours were being achieved. Seventy-five percent productivity, or six hours a day, was optimal without going into overtime. In any event, overtime would only add to overhead and increase the contribution required.

I experienced a fleeting sense of failure, with all its consequences for the contractor and the loss of face for the accountant, who had gone out on a limb to involve me with his clients.

I recall standing there as the seconds ticked away, wondering what the solution could be. To gain more time, I put out a feeler: "Are you achieving your quoted times, or are you running over?"

"Some run over, some run under, but on average they match up," he replied.

"Who does the quoting?" I asked

"The estimator," he replied.

"How does he work out his times?"

"He has a pretty sophisticated software package that he works from."

"How does he track actual times against target?" I queried.

"All the time sheets are fed to him. He records the times taken and uses them to update or develop times for all types of work."

"Does he carry out any work or method study of the jobs to check if they are being done efficiently or otherwise?"

He laughed at the thought. "He hasn't been out of the office for the past five years to my knowledge. He's too flat-out running his neck of the woods. No, he relies on the time sheets, and that is sensible enough. The men are fairly good with their times; we keep an eye on them."

"Do you remember me talking about HCL—Human Comfort Level—at the seminar?" I asked.

"Yes I do, but I don't think it applies in our case," he replied.

I reminded him of this important point. "Where no plan or target or budget has been established, there is a tendency for effort to sink to human comfort level, or HCL. If there has been no reassessment of times for jobs, the tendency will inevitably lead to an expansion of those times. Imperceptible maybe, but inevitable!" My confidence surged as I glimpsed a potential solution.

"What are you saying?" he queried.

"Well, if your estimator has been relying on time sheets to update times per job and using them in the quoting, those times will have blown out over the years. It is characteristic of time sheets."

He asked, "You mean we are overquoting the time a job should take?"

"Exactly!"

"Well, what do we do? We don't have time to work- or method-study the jobs. We would be out of business before we got started!"

I wrote $6 on the whiteboard and divided by $46 to get 13%.

"I suggest that for the moment, you get the estimator to take 13 percent off all times quoted and leave the target contribution or TARI at $46. For example, if you have job estimated to take 100 hours, cut the estimate to 87 hours."

"But why 13 percent?"

"Because that's the difference between getting a contribution of $40 compared with $46 an hour. You believe you can win quotes at $40 an hour based on current time estimates. For example, a job estimated to take 100 hours at $40 an hour will amount to $4,000. But the job will also amount to $4,000 if you complete it in 87 hours at $46 an hour."

I wrote on the whiteboard:

$$100 \text{ hours} \times \$40 = \$4,000$$
$$87 \text{ hours} \times \$46 = \$4,002$$

For a moment or two, he was nonplussed. "I don't know if we can do it. After all, the men have a good idea of how long a job should take."

"I'd be surprised if they track the times against the quote," I replied. "How much do they know about the quoted hours at the outset of a job?"

He shook his head. "I guess they don't. They just go to a job pretty much according to the schedule we put out at the beginning of each week."

"So if you want this to work for you, the men need to be aware of the targeted times."

"I guess that will lead to designing some sort of incentive system?" he queried with raised eyebrows.

"Whatever happens, don't even think of an incentive system until you get everyone to accept the idea of completing a job in the targeted hours. And even then, any incentive should be based on what comes in over and above targeted net profit."[6]

When speaking with the accountant some months later, he told me his client was on track to meet the targeted net profit. It appeared the owner had taken a more active role, splitting the 20 technicians into four teams of five each to hold weekly action meetings at which they reviewed results of the previous week, discussed the scheduled work for the week ahead, and noted their responses on Action Sheets for review and follow-up by the owner.[7]

Regular contact with the owner, as well as the estimator and accountant, had the effect of melding a disparate group of individuals into a team with a clear focus on the target they were aiming to achieve.

Case Comment

The two keys of activity and gross profit contribution at the heart of every business are clearly demonstrated in this case study. If the desired contribution rate is unachievable, the alternative is to review the level of billable or output activity.

If the level of billable activity cannot be achieved, the alternative is to review the contribution rate, bearing in mind it is also possible to improve net profit by reducing the cost of materials or parts used as per the example in Table 5-3.

---

[6]Table 1-2 illustrates a simple format for tracking weekly results for comparison with target.
[7]The owner made a point of sitting in with each team for 10 minutes or so, and he ensured the estimator and accountant did the same from time to time—not so long that individual members of the team would be inhibited in freely expressing their views, but long enough to make them realize he was there to help and not hinder.

Table 5-3. Unit Contribution and Material Cost

Example	Sale Price A ($)	Materials B ($)	Contribution C = (A − B) ($)	% D = C ÷ A	Units (Hours) E	Average per Unit F ($)
1	3,500	1,500	2,000	57	50	40
2	3,500	1,350	2,150	61	50	43
3	3,500	1,250	2,250	64	50	45

As an instrument for reviewing activity, time sheets are potentially useful but only if maintained accurately and compared with times quoted for a job. What really matters is what goes on between the time of signing on and signing off.

Our research shows that time sheets are notoriously inaccurate as a guide to productivity and efficiency. With few exceptions, times are seldom compared with times quoted.

Work-study covers the overall method as well as the timing of jobs. This case study is typical of businesses developed from one-person startups where proprietors work for themselves and awareness of how long a job should take is based primarily on their own input.

As a business grows, taking on more personnel and generating more activity, the proprietor becomes increasingly distanced from the shop floor or fieldwork, and times inevitably blow out.

In the case of this business, it was one thing to point the way by cutting back on estimated times, but it was quite another to make it work. Without the week-by-week discipline of action meetings in conjunction with Action Sheets, implementing the desired change would have fallen by the wayside. It bears out the well-worn saying of "20% genius, 80% implementation," and is something that the following real-life case study illustrates.

CHAPTER 6

Horticultural Equipment Proprietor's Moment of Truth

Struggling to repay the bank, the proprietor blamed himself for going into debt against his better instincts. However, the debt was not the cause of his problem at all.

"I borrowed from the bank to buy a steel guillotine to save me having to take the steel across town every time I wanted to get it cut. And now I can't make the payments."[1] Max was a man who hated the thought of borrowing because of the very problem he now found himself facing. The specter of potential disaster loomed large on his horizon.

---

[1] Steel is delivered to the factory in plates and rolls, depending on thickness, and needs cutting to suit the work at hand.

Chapter 6 | Horticultural Equipment Proprietor's Moment of Truth

He was making a variety of horticultural machines for polishing and packing fruit. The business had developed after he retired from a career in tool making in order to purchase an avocado orchard. At the end of his first year on the orchard, when the time came to wash, polish, and pack the fruit, he was unable to hire the necessary equipment or gain access to the local horticultural cooperative plant.

So he bought, cut, and welded steel, and mechanized his own plant. It was compact and highly efficient—so much so, that demand for like models began to flow, to the point where he built a large shed and hired labor. At the time of our meeting, the business was several years down the track, employing nine people in production with overseas exports well under way.

"Are your people busy?" I asked.

"Flat out," he responded, giving an answer I had come to expect 9 times out of 10.

"How do you know?" I pressed.

"They are good men. They like to live and work in the countryside; their children go to school here; their wives want to stay here; they don't belong to a union."

It was not difficult to see why they liked living in the area: it was bathed with bright sunshine and refreshed by adequate rainfall; was rich in volcanic soils that enabled flowers, fruit, and lush pastures to proliferate; and was a short drive from endless miles of golden sands and rolling Pacific Ocean surf.

"I can understand they like living here, Max, but how do you know they are working productively?"

"What do you mean?"

"I mean, how do you know they are flat out?"

"The window in my office looks over the factory and I can see them at work every time I look out." He omitted to mention he was away much of the time attending trade exhibitions, servicing customers, and spearheading a thrust into overseas markets.

"Can we look at the output for the past year?" I asked, getting away from what threatened to be a talkfest in order to glance at the financial statements. They revealed no more than conventional sales and expenses and made no reference to productivity.

In response to my request for something more helpful, he produced a pile of well-thumbed invoice books containing handwritten carbon copies of invoices.

We laboriously extracted each product sold, noting the cost of materials used and the estimated hours on a sheet of paper (Table 6-1).

Improving Profit

Table 6-1. Identifying Billed Hours in Last Year's Output

Description of Product	Number of Products Sold	Hours to Produce a Single Product	Total Units (Hours)
Avocado Packer	30	60	1,800
Nutcracker	16	40	640
Lychee Picker	20	50	1,000
Punnet Seeder[2]	14	80	1,120
Total	**80**	**230**	**4,560**

"You have nine in full-time production, working how many hours?" I asked

"Forty hours a week each," he said.

"Any overtime?"

"Yes, about four hours a week each. It gives them a bit of extra."

"And would they get four weeks' annual leave plus a week's sick leave on full pay?" I asked.

"Yes, plus 10 days public holidays," he replied.

"So with 4 weeks' holiday plus the equivalent of 2 weeks of public holidays plus a week's sick leave, they would work 45 weeks for 52 weeks' pay?"

Max nodded in agreement.

"Well 44 hours a week works out at roughly 1,980 hours per full-time employee in production hours, or 17,820 total for nine employees." I noted the figures on a whiteboard (Table 6-2).

Table 6-2. Calculating Paid Hours in Production

A	Hours per Week per Employee	40 hours
B	Overtime per Week per Employee	4 hours
C = (A + B)	Total Paid Hours per Week	44 hours
D = (C × 52)	Total Paid Hours per Year per Employee	2,288 hours
E = (D × 9)	Total Paid Hours for 9 employees	20,592 hours
F = (C × 7 Weeks × 9)	Hours on Annual Leave, Public Holidays, Sick Leave	2,772 hours
G = (E − F)	Hours at Work	17,820 hours

---

[2] A punnet is a small cup—usually made of plastic—that holds enough soil to enable a seed to grow to a certain height, following which the embryonic plant can be transferred either to another, larger punnet or directly to a garden or field as the case may be.

Chapter 6 | Horticultural Equipment Proprietor's Moment of Truth

"Yes, I see that," he said. "But so what?"

"Well, it means that you are paying some 20,592 hours for the production team to work 17,820 hours, of which you bill 4,560 hours."

That works out as close to 25% or two hours charged out on a typical eight-hour day (Table 6-3).[3]

Table 6-3. Pinpointing Productivity

A	Hours Tracked in Output	4,560 hours
B	Hours at Work	17,820 hours
C = (A ÷ B × 100)	Productivity	25%
D = (25% × 8.8 hours)	Output per Person per 8.8-Hour Day	2.2 hours

Max jumped up and exclaimed, "There must be more invoice books somewhere!" He went off to check desks, drawers, and filing cabinets.

However, there were no more invoices and the invoiced prices for the products listed added up very close to the year's sales as spelled out in the financials.

"How is this possible?" he asked when he had settled down again. "None of them are slackers."

He picked up the financial statements, which compared last year with the previous year. "How come the sales have not dropped?" he asked with a twinge of doubt about the prognosis creeping into his voice.

"You mentioned you had raised your prices, and the high returns flowing from the new punnet seeder have been masking low productivity. The combination of falling output and increased expenses has put pressure on your ability to repay the loan."

"I don't understand it," he reiterated.

"It's fairly normal, I assure you. You got things started; you worked out the times for each type of unit produced and you priced the jobs accordingly. The business grew and you found yourself attending trade shows and exhibitions, installing the units on properties, servicing the breakdowns, hiring new staff, interviewing sales reps, collecting debts, paying bills, and spending hours on new developments. Regardless of how hard you tried, you lost touch with production throughput.

---

[3]Based on a 44-hour week, the production team was at work 8.8 hours a day. However, 8.8 hours a day at the workplace does not mean they are all available for working on products. There will be time set aside for cleanup, equipment maintenance, and inevitable downtimes. Billable hours for this type of business should be closer to 70% of available hours. In this case, 70% × 17,820 hours = 12,474 hours.

"And it's not that the men are slacking, either," I continued. "They are pacing themselves. Maybe the job that can be done in ten minutes is now done in twenty or more. You look around and they are all busy, but they have slowed down, knowing they will run out of work by the end of the day or week. Bring the work in and they'll speed up."[4]

Max said, "How is it that my accountant doesn't tell me these things? He told me if he gives me regular figures, I could not go wrong. Now I see the position is serious even though sales dollars are up on last year. What use are these figures to me?" He threw the statements back into the bottom drawer.

"I'm sorry to have to say it, Max, but if there is a textbook written that teaches how to identify levels of productive activity and relate it to a financial contribution in a practical sense, the accounting profession hasn't advertised it." I explained that current financial statements are simply not geared to point out that his production team achieved two hours of output for eight hours of pay. I then told him that quarterly statements such as those he was getting were more helpful than annual statements, but they arrived a month after the period to which they referred, and the management information they provide was extremely limited.

"In any event," I said, "by the time they arrive, it is a bit late to remedy what has already occurred. That's why you need to track progress weekly. That way, you can be in a position to make corrections before small problems become big ones."

"How would I get them weekly?" he asked, "The accountant's on my back enough as it is to get information every three months."

"Collecting the information necessary to give you the focus you need is not difficult," I said. "All you need is complete a summary sheet of invoices once a week. After all, you only have one, two, or three invoices at the most to make out."

I instructed him to note the invoice number of the sale, the sale price, the cost price of materials, and the hours quoted or established for the unit or units sold. I concluded, "You make sure it is filled in every Friday and add the total onto the previous totals so you keep a running check."

I sketched out a format to give him the idea, (Table 6-4).

---

[4] During a break, I went into the plant and spoke with the foreman. He said he was well aware of the order book and what work lay ahead. He admitted that when the order book showed few if any orders were lined up, the production team slowed down so they didn't run out of work completely. Obviously, Max was overstaffed for the output being generated, but he didn't know it. The question thus becomes, "Why not adjust staff numbers to meet the level of work flowing through the factory?" It had taken Max several years to build a loyal and dedicated team able to cope with a variety of machines, some of them highly technical. The last thought in his mind would be to lay one or more people off. The demand for his products went through highs and lows with seasonal weather playing a significant role. When harvests were poor, demand faded and vice versa.

Chapter 6 | Horticultural Equipment Proprietor's Moment of Truth

Table 6-4. Invoice Analysis for Week Ending _____ [5]

Invoice Number	Price Net of Tax ($) A	Materials Used ($) B	Gross Profit Contribution ($) C = A − B	Gross Profit Contribution[6] (%) D = (C ÷ A)	Units in Hours E	Average GPC per Unit ($) F = (C ÷ E)	Target per Unit
132	5,000	2,000	3,000	60	30	100	100
138	12,000	6,000	6,000	50	55	109	100
145	9,000	4,000	5,000	56	60	83	100
Week	26,000	12,000	14,000	54	133	105	100

Max said, "But I've got orders that take several weeks to put together."

"That's no problem," I said. "You only note the sales made. Work in progress is going on all the time and eventually translates into sales."

"What about the time spent on research and development of new machines and so on?"

"Do you use the production team to help you?"

"No, not really," said Max. "I might use the foreman occasionally. I usually wait until they have knocked off for the day before I get down to it."

"In that case, there is no need to allocate some of their hours to R&D. So let's look ahead at the likely expenses for next year."

We worked our way down the list using his guesstimates. Excluding the cost of materials and outsourced work, the expenses totaled $630,000.

"What shall we put down for profit, bearing in mind you broke even and covered expenses on 4,560 hours charged out? Just think of the potential if you can charge out 9,000 hours, which is close to 50% of 17,820 hours!"

The thought seemed to cheer him up, and we targeted $270,000 net profit to arrive at a gross profit target of $900,000. We divided this by the targeted 9,000 chargeable hours to get a target average gross profit contribution of $100.

---

[5] Table 6-4 is purely an example for Max. However, it illustrates a case where the average contribution per hour exceeds the TARI benchmark, and where billed hours fall hours behind target, suggesting the products are profitable enough in themselves, but not enough of them are heading out the door.

[6] Gross Profit Contribution: After deducting the cost of materials purchased from a supplier, the amount left over is the contribution toward covering expenses and profit. Sometimes this is referred to as "added value."

"Assuming a 45-week year and a target of 9,000 chargeable hours, you need 200 hours per week charged into product at an average gross contribution of $100 an hour," I said (Table 6-5). "We refer to that average as the target average rate index or TARI, so it will not be confused with a cost or a price. It is a benchmark against which you can compare the gross profit contribution per hour from any product or job."

Table 6-5. Planning Ahead

A	Target Expenses	$630,000
B	Target Profit	$270,000
C =(A + B)	Target Contribution	$900,000
D	Target Billable Units	9,000 hours
E = (C ÷ D)	Target Average (TARI)	$100
F	Working Weeks	45 weeks
G = (D ÷ F)	Weekly Average Billable Units	200 hours
H = (E × G)	Weekly Average Contribution	$20,000

Realizing this was a lot to take in during one session, I pulled out an Action Sheet to note the key points that had been covered and get agreement on who was to do what by when (Table 6-6).[7]

Table 6-6. Action Sheet

Item	Action	Who	When
Invoices	Extract the contribution from each invoice weekly and divide by the production hours to identify the contribution	Max and BK	7/10
Tracking results	Track the invoices weekly and accumulatively for comparison with TARI and the target billable hours	Max and BK	7/10
Meetings	Commence weekly meeting with key staff to review previous week's performance and plan week ahead	Max, BK, HG	7/17
Quoting	Compare the contribution per hour of quotes with the TARI benchmark before submitting quote	Max and JK	7/10

Present at meeting: Max, BK, HG, KC

Without input from his key employees, there was no way Max would be in a position to follow through with implementing the changes.

---

[7]Chapter 22 illustrates the powerful impact of an Action Sheet in operation.

Chapter 6 | Horticultural Equipment Proprietor's Moment of Truth

Eight years passed, and apart from an occasional phone call, we lost touch. Then Max's wife rang to ask for help. She said profit had steadily increased over the years to $400,000, but that had fallen to a loss of $150,000 during the past year.

It seemed that when Max had semi-retired and handed control to a newly appointed general manager, the business began to decline, reaching the point where Max needed to borrow heavily against the security of his house and property in order to pay suppliers demanding cash payment for materials.

It did not take long to find out that comparison of invoices with TARI along with weekly feedback had been discarded in favor of software the general manager had used during previous employment with a major corporation.

The process of monitoring performance weekly and accumulatively in the CBA format recommenced, and 12 months down the track, the business was slowly correcting the situation.

The key to achieving the turnaround lay in comparing invoices with the TARI benchmark at the time of quoting as well as comparing actual results with target each week—on the grounds that it was possible to catch up on a bad week but much more difficult to catch up on a bad month. Table 6-7 presents a format to capture data for the week as well as the weeks to date.

Table 6-7. Performance Summary Ending Week 6

Day	Sales ($) A	Cost of Materials ($) B	Gross Profit ($) C = A − B	Gross Profit (%) D = C ÷ A	Number of Hours E	Average Gross Profit per Hour($) F = C ÷ E
1	6,000	3,200	2,800	47	40	70
5	28,800	14,800	14,000	49	135	104
Total	34,800	18,000	16,800	48[8]	175	96
Total b/f	220,000	108,000	112,000	51.0	1,098	102
Total c/f[9]	254,800	126,000	128,800	50.5	1,273	101
Target	240,000	120,000	120,000	50	1,200	100
Variance	+14,800	+6,000	+8,800	+0.5	+73	+1

---

[8] 48% is the overall average for the week.
[9] b/f = brought forward; c/f = carried forward.

Case Comment

Max was no ordinary toolmaker turned manufacturer. His machines became a byword for quality and durability. His computerized punnet filling and seeding lines, supplemented by robotic arms to transfer embryonic plants from small to larger punnets, were sought after by countries as far apart as China, Saudi Arabia, Germany, and the United States.

His production manager was a highly intelligent engineer who synchronized the purchase orders for just-in-time delivery of materials and parts fully itemized at the completion of the design and coordinated the workflow through the plant. He was a cheerful and cooperative team member.

The marketing manager, who had an engineering background, specialized in quotations for the larger, highly computerized seeding units in demand by nurseries, and followed through with arrangements for on-site establishment and support by the in-house team.

The accounts were handled by a skilled bookkeeper under the supervision of the firm's external accounting practice.

For several years running, Max's business was awarded "Export Business of the Year" in the state's small and medium-sized business category.

It was a talented team working creatively and in harmony with one another, but a team that nevertheless felt the need to employ a general manager who, in the words of Max, "would bring the loose ends together and provide direction."

As it turned out, the general manager's experience was gained in the corporate world, from which he had retired early to enjoy a more relaxed lifestyle away from the city.

He introduced methods and systems that cost money and created information overkill. Over the subsequent years, the firm started to lose heavily. Max mortgaged his home and land to provide cash to continue. By the time I responded to the cry for help from Max's wife, the GM had gracefully retired.

For a business to sustain the rigors involved with survival and growth, it needs a focal point upon which management can agree, and around which the functioning departments are able to operate, like spokes in a wheel—a business wheel.

I saw that a business can be likened to a wheel turning according to the level of billable units of activity at the hub, with the spokes representing various functions such as personnel, production, marketing administration, finance, IT systems, and so forth.[10]

---

[10] For an illustration of how 12 senior managers viewed their businesses in a wheel format, see Appendix D.

Chapter 6 | Horticultural Equipment Proprietor's Moment of Truth

For a wheel to operate in a balanced way with a minimum of friction, the spokes need to be of equal length. Should one or more of the spokes protrude ahead of the others, the impact is transmitted to the hub.

If the wheel is targeted to move at an agreed speed (units of output) matching available resources (contribution), the extent of any change in speed will be reflected at the hub by

1. comparing actual unit-contribution with TARI on an invoice-by-invoice basis and
2. comparison with the overall weekly and accumulative target.

Max has now retired but the business continues, closely attuned to the need for a sustained focus on the hub.

It is the sustained focus on movement at the hub (output and gross profit contribution per unit of output) that tends to become self-fulfilling, not only for manufacturing or service-oriented sectors, but for wholesale and retail business as well, as the following real-life case study in Chapter 7 illustrates.

CHAPTER 7

Wholesaler Nets $2.5M in 10+ Months

A management buyout of a company, being sold for lack of profitable performance, illustrates what can happen when targets are broken into digestible proportions

During a daylong workshop with 20 clients of a coastal accounting practice, I came across a business supplying ships with provisions ranging from anchovies to anchors. The proprietor, himself an ex–seagoing captain, responded warmly to the concept underlying CBA[1] and asked if I would run a workshop for his five branch managers.

Over the next year or so, I conducted workshops every four months. We analyzed past results and planned ongoing performance, giving managers an opportunity to explain their successes as well as their failures.

---

[1] Contribution Based Activity.

By year's end, while the improvement in overall performance was apparent, it was not until the business was taken over by a major corporate group, and another 21 branches joined the 5 existing branches, that the extent of change became obvious. The managers of the existing branches were far ahead of their peers in grasping the essentials of what made a business tick.

The takeover represented but 1 of 300 or more takeovers by the major corporation, which specialized in improving business performance by demanding improved accounting systems and reporting procedures that filled 150 pages of a monthly report for the board.

Three years subsequent to the takeover, the corporation went belly-up. The CEO of the enlarged provisioning group, the ex-captain, approached me to help with a management buyout from the bankruptcy administrators. Upon successful completion of the buyout, I agreed to take on the role of chairman until the company settled into its stride.

Sales were around $50 million, with gross profit contribution running at a low 20% of sales and a net profit of nil.

Calling a meeting of senior executives to work out a strategy for the year ahead, I asked, "What is the average sale?" and looked around the table. There was silence and a shuffling of feet.

Finally the general manager spoke up. "There's no such thing in this business," he said, somewhat indulgently.

"Why do you say that?" I asked.

"Well, a major customer like one of the Queens might order $150,000 worth at once, or we'll get a tug boat ordering bread and milk for $50. No way can there be an average sale in this business."

"Well, there's one thing for sure," I replied, "if we don't know the average sale, we certainly can't improve it."

I recounted an example of a typical hardware store with some 7,000 product lines, ranging from $1,000 chainsaws to 50-cent packets of screws. The contribution[2] per average sale was $20 and once it had been identified, the daily average achieved would be noted in large characters on the whiteboard in the employee's staff room. It provided a daily update and helped sustain focus on where the rubber meets the road.

I said, "As we don't even have a record of the number of sales made, we need to start tracking the sales and gross profit contribution per sale for every vessel supplied. In time, that will build up a more accurate picture."

---

[2]*Contribution*, normally known as *gross profit contribution*, refers to the amount left over after deducting the cost of goods obtained from a supplier.

As the weeks passed, information from branches was processed and sent back to each branch in a format that could be pinned up on lunchroom notice boards. The results for each representative were highlighted showing the number of sales made and the average contribution achieved, both for the preceding week and accumulatively for the weeks to date (Table 7-1).

Table 7-1. Branch and Rep Results, Week Ending _____

Rep	Sales for Week ($) A	Gross Profit ($) B	Margin % C = (B ÷ A)	Sales Total to Date ($) D	Gross Profit to Date ($) E	Gross Profit % to Date F = (E ÷ D)	No. of Sales to Date G	Average Gross Profit per Sale to Date H = (E ÷ G)
RC	20,631	3,920	19	139,263	26,460	19	7	3,780
PH	8,928	1,875	21	136,190	28,600	21	6	4,767
LT	20,800	4,160	20	124,700	24,940	20	5	4,988
DS	15,474	2,940	19	131,428	27,600	21	5	5,520
Total	65,833	12,895	19	531,581	107,600	20	23	4,678

Analysis of past sales quickly established the average sale had been in the region of $5,000, and focus shifted from vague generalizations about how to improve an existing overall 20% contribution for $50 million in sales, to a contribution of 25% on a $5,000 sale.

In reality the $5,000 was a statistical average and actual sales ranged widely. By refocusing on a manageable average sale of $5,000, it was possible for management and representatives to target the real objective, which was to improve the contribution margin from the equivalent of $1,000 to $1,250 per average sale.[3]

I pressed for a target of 25% contribution per sale with recording to commence immediately.

It was a question that became the focus of subsequent management meetings, resulting in simple and achievable objectives that could be carried out in each branch.

Within two months, reports filtered back from branches revealing different methods adopted to improve the gross profit per sale.

One northern branch, handling coal vessels, took brochures from the local jeweler on board the ships and sold opals to the crew, increasing the average contribution by $300 a sale.

---

[3] 20% of $5,000 = $1,000, 25% = $1,250. In other words, it represented an improved contribution of $250 per sale.

Chapter 7 | Wholesaler Nets $2.5M in 10+ Months

Another branch made a deal with the local video outlet and sold videos to the crew, increasing the average contribution by $200 per sale.

The previous ordering system, in which 60 representatives wrote out the order and the head office completed the invoice, with no one in between identifying the contribution margin, was changed so that each representative worked out the contribution margin at the time the order was made out.

This in turn called for lessons on how to ensure a minimum contribution of 25%—while still taking account of a possible 5% discount for early settlement. Table 7-2 provides an illustration.

Table 7-2. Example of Pricing

Cost Price of the Order	=	$1,000
Assumed Discount on Sale Price for Early Settlement	=	5%
Required Contribution Margin	=	25%[4]
Sale Price Calculation	=	(Cost Price + 33%) × 105.264%[5]
($1,000 + 33%)	=	$1,330
($1,330 × 105.264%)	=	$1,400

Note: 25% gross profit contribution margin on sale = 33% markup on cost

The change for improved contributions flowed once each branch pinned up the weekly and cumulative results of each representative, resulting in a focus on contribution rather than sale volume as had previously been the case.

With the increased gross profit contribution flowing directly to the bottom line, and gross profit contribution margins continuing to climb with the support of improved buying and focusing on items that attracted higher margins, net profit rose steeply, in turn strengthening the cash flow.

Quarterly management workshops imparted additional input, training branch management in planning, targeting, and monitoring performance; providing a means of sharing marketing skills; developing more effective and timely collection of the proceeds; and sharpening techniques of purchasing to reduce costs and control inventory.

---

[4] A 25% contribution margin on the sale price equates to a 33% markup on cost price. For example, 25% on a sale price of $100 = $25; a 33% markup of $75 = $100.
[5] A discount of 5% on the sale price requires a markup of 5.264%.

From the time of the management buyout to the end of the financial year—a period covering 10.5 months—the average gross profit per sale increased by $250, which on 10,000 sales, resulted in a net profit of $2.5 million.

The success attracted the attention of stockbrokers, and within 18 months from the time of buyout, the company was listed on the stock exchange, providing a handsome paper gain for the shareholders as well as additional cash for funding expansion.

Case Comment

It was at this point that I stepped down from the chairman's role, handing the job over to one of the three newly appointed nonexecutive directors.

Given the need to report to the stock exchange and deal with the more burdensome regulatory matters of a listed company, the board in its wisdom replaced the existing chief accountant with a more sophisticated company secretary from a major accounting firm.

Unfamiliar with the software that had been introduced to handle the week-by-week reports to and from the branches, he dispensed with them and reverted to the traditional monthly reporting practice contained in a 120-page Board Pack, completed three weeks after the month to which the contents referred.

The branches continued to send in their weekly reports, but the head office merely filed them without providing any feedback of results for posting on the branch notice board. Within six months, the gross profit margin fell from a high of 28% to a terminal 20%.

Lack of focus on where the rubber meets the road brought the company close to negative profit, and within a year of listing, I was asked to return as chairman.

Chasing an annual target of, say, $50 million can only be achieved by small steps, with each day taking care of itself. Thus the importance of focusing on gross profit contribution sale by sale and the number of sales week by week.

The average sale of $5,000 was purely a statistic. It is unlikely there ever was such a sale, but it was eminently more digestible than focusing on $50 million.

The point is that $5,000 could be comprehended and focused on by the branch managers, although each branch had a different average sale depending on the size of the vessel loading at the port.

The simple objectives called for each branch to target a number of sales together with an average gross profit per sale. It then became a matter of developing ways and means of achieving increased added value per sale, a process that drew on the combined input of branch personnel, who responded accordingly to achieve outstanding results.

It was also revealing to hear from the branch managers at the quarterly workshops the different methods reps used to boost the added value per sale, knowing their results would be published on the notice board and promulgated in the company newsletter.

An interesting aspect of this case was the extensive monthly reporting system that had been established under the previous owners, a multinational group with several hundred subsidiaries, each providing a monthly Board Pack covering traditional financial statements, aging of accounts receivables, details of staffing, pertinent comments from each branch, and so forth. But there was nothing about number of sales made, average sale, or gross profit per sale, whether overall or by branch or representative.[6]

Following my return as chairman, the system of weekly feedback of number of sales and average gross profit per sale was reinstated, much to the initial skepticism of some board members. However, the time came when one of the first questions at the commencement of board meetings was, "How are we going with TARI?"

The following real-life case study of a small retailer illustrates what can happen when focus is sustained day by day on the two key drivers of activity—number of sales and $ rate (gross profit contribution per sale).

---

[6]Table 1-2 in Chapter 1 illustrates a simple format for tracking weekly results for comparison with a target.

CHAPTER 8

Jeweler's Changed Focus Turns Red into Black

Dependent on passing-tourist trade, this jeweler found it impossible to do more than cover costs, let alone make a profit

I was conducting interviews with clients of a well-established accounting practice, following a client seminar the previous day. The owner of a jewelry shop had requested an interview session.

He was having trouble. Sales volume was up last year, but the bottom line showed a loss. Discounting had been too high. Given its location on a 20-minute tourist stopover, it was perhaps understandable that the focus tended to be on a sale at any price. Nevertheless, it was thought that next year, things would be better because of a potential pickup in tourism.

Chapter 8 | Jeweler's Changed Focus Turns Red into Black

"I don't know why I put my name down for an interview, really," he said. "Our problem can only be solved by more tourist buses. So how can you help us?"

"I can't help you with the jewelry side of the business," I replied, "but I can help you with the management side if you care to cooperate in the TARI process that I spoke about yesterday."

"What's that?" the husband and wife said in unison, despite the fact I had explained it at length during the client seminar the previous evening.

"It's essentially a matter of focusing on two key performance indicators that have been found to make all the difference between success and mediocre performance in business."

"Tell us more," said the husband.

"Well," I asked, "as a first step, perhaps you can tell me your average sale?"

"Average sale?" He turned to his wife. "What do you reckon?" She shook her head. "I guess about $30, more or less."

"What about the average gross profit contribution per sale?"

"Well," the jeweler said, "I suppose if the average sale is $30 and the markup is 100%, the average gross profit would be $15. But why ask?"

"Because the $15 gross profit is the contribution toward covering your expenses and profit," I replied. "The other $15 covers the cost of purchases and, as you are in business for yourself and not for your suppliers, it's what's left over after the cost of purchases that matters."

"I don't get the drift," said the wife. "What's the point of knowing the average gross profit?"[1]

"Because," I replied, "it's difficult to improve on an amount that you don't know."

"Hmmm," she murmured.

"You can get a close approximation by looking at the cash register sales and markups per day, for a selection of, say, six days that you believe to be representative of sales and contribution," I suggested.[2]

---

[1]*Gross profit, gross profit contribution,* or simply *contribution* all refer to the amount left over from a sale after deducting the cost of goods. It is a "contribution" toward covering expenses and profit. Obviously, contribution will be impacted by discounting and/or low numbers of sales.

[2]*Markup* refers to the amount added on to the cost price to get the sales price. As a percentage on cost, it is referred to as markup. *Gross profit contribution* refers to a percentage of the sale price. In dollar terms, gross profit and markup refer to the same amount. For example, a ring costing $100 is marked up 100% to sell for $200. The gross profit contribution of $100 is calculated by dividing the cost price by the sale price and pressing the percentage button ($100 ÷ $200 = 50%).

With some reluctance, the jeweler agreed to forward the sample information the following week.

By the time we met again, the accountant had prepared the analysis (Table 8-1).

Table 8-1. Analysis of a Representative Sample of Sales[3]

Day	Sale Price ($) A	Cost of Goods Sold ($) B	Gross Profit Contribution ($) C = (A − B)	Gross Profit Margin (%) D = (C ÷ A)	Number of Sales E	Average Gross Profit Contribution per Sale ($) F = (C ÷ E)
5/6	1,100	715	385	35	26	15.00
5/10	1,400	868	532	38	59	9.00
5/13	1,250	725	525	42	46	11.50
5/16	1,500	900	600	40	46	13.00
5/21	1,360	898	462	34	32	14.50
5/27	1,290	800	490	38	49	10.00
Total	7,900	4,906	2,994	38	258[4]	11.60

Surprised to see the range in gross profit per sale, the jeweler asked, "Where do we go from here?"

I said, "Well, let's start tracking from tomorrow by comparing the average gross profit contribution with a target average contribution per sale. We call it TARI, short for target average rate index. It is a benchmark."

The jeweler nodded, and I continued. "All you need to do is note the sales, cost of goods sold, and the number of sales on this format and e-mail it in once a week. The accountant will input it to the software and return the results back the next day. That will give you an up-to-date fix on where you are compared with target."

---

[3] It is worth noting that the sample analysis could have extracted the number of items sold per sale, seeing as a sale frequently includes more than one item. In the case of comparing two or more retail outlets of similar products, the items per sale can be a very useful comparison of merchandising techniques. Volume of sales can be similar, but gross profit per sale noticeably different, because one outlet is more conscious of the added value per sale than the other.

[4] The average sale in Table 8-1 is $30.62 ($7,900 ÷ 258); the average number of sales per day is 43 (258 ÷ 6 days).

The accountant handed him several sheets preprinted with the format.

"What's my target, then?" the jeweler asked.

"Good question," I replied. "We need to decide that before you go."

After projecting the likely expenses and adding a desirable net profit for the year ahead, we got to the point of dividing the resulting target gross profit by an estimated number of sales to arrive at a TARI (Table 8-2).

Table 8-2. Planning and Targeting Ahead

A	Target Total Expenses	$125,000
B	Target Net Profit	$75,000
C = (A + B)	Target Gross Profit Contribution	$200,000
D	Target No. Sales	15,000
E = (C ÷ D)	TARI = $200,000 ÷ 15,000	$13.33
F	Target Contribution Margin %	40%[5]
G = (C ÷ F)	Target Sales = 200,000 ÷ 40%	$500,000
H = (G – C)	Target Cost of Goods Sold	$300,000

"What number of sales shall we target?" I asked.

Raising his eyebrows, the jeweler looked at his wife. "What do you think?" he asked her. "I think we'll hit $500,000 in revenue this year, but how many individual sales?"

"Well," she said, "depending on the tourist buses, some weeks we would have over 500 and some weeks under 200. I wouldn't really know until I checked the figures."

I pointed out the sample analysis in Table 8-1 indicated a daily average of 43 sales.[6] "Assuming you are open for business for, say, 350 days of the year, 43 multiplied by 350 is 15,050 sales. So let's target 15,000 sales to start with. Once we get some feedback we can adjust targets as required to achieve the desired bottom line. As you can see, if our guesses are about right, we'll need an average contribution per sale of about $13.33 to cover expenses and provide a nice profit."

The accountant reached for the Action Sheet (Table 8-3) and began to spell out who was to do what by when.

---

[5] 40% gross profit margin increases the previous GP margin of 38%.
[6] 258 ÷ 6 days = 43.

Table 8-3. Action Sheet

Date	Item	Action	Who	When
11/7	Tracking Results	Record sales, cost of goods sold, and number of sales daily	KG	11/8
11/7	Tracking Results	E-mail weekly summary to accountant for input to software	KG	11/14
11/7	Review	Meet to discuss results	KG/JD/BS	11/21

Present at meeting: JD, MD, BS, KC

I asked the accountant to let me know how things developed. However, it was several months before we had occasion to speak, and it was then he told me the jeweler had turned the corner and had in fact achieved a contribution per sale of closer to $14.

Always intrigued at how managers achieve nice boosts to contribution, I asked if he would get the jeweler to give his perceptions of what had made the difference.

"I'll try," he said, "though I doubt we will get a response." But as it happened, a response did come from the accountant within a week or two.

The accountant told me over the phone, "He likes the idea of monitoring progress weekly and is currently running ahead of target. The reasons he gives are as follows."

The accountant started to paraphrase an e-mail he was reading:

"Likes the idea of having a yardstick by which to gauge performance on weekly basis. It gives his management function some structure. Information obtained has assisted in:

- Developing product mix (to improve gross profit)
- Formulating a pricing policy better reflective of costs
- Obtaining better feedback on the effectiveness of marketing activity
- Obtaining better feedback on effectiveness of sales staff
- Obtaining a better understanding of the cycles that affect his business

"He believes 'the process has been valuable and helped increase profit and give direction.'"

Chapter 8 | Jeweler's Changed Focus Turns Red into Black

I subsequently learned the jeweler had stood up at a client taxation seminar held by the accountant and spoken enthusiastically of the help he had received.

"It was a bit embarrassing, really," the accountant explained with a smile in his voice.

Case Comment

I was fortunate to interview this jeweler in conjunction with an accountant familiar with the CBA approach. He did not push for analysis of historical data to analyze past performance. He knew from experience the data would be fragmented, tax oriented, and unreliable as a guide to targeting future performance.

He was also well aware it was best to start with a sample of sales as a basis for planning ahead, and then move on to capture actual data going forward, so the real picture would emerge over the ensuing weeks.

The sample does not pinpoint productivity in the same way as in a manufacturing or service business, where the key activity relates more to man or machine hours. Where data is available, it is possible to make comparisons with other similar retail businesses to assess staff effectiveness. Known as Interfirm Comparison, the data will normally provide an indication of sales per person employed.

Many retailers maintain records of number of sales made and can easily derive their average sale. However, there are numerous occasions on which discounts are applied in an attempt to increase the number of sales and boost the overall contribution without realizing the overall impact on the bottom line.

Caught up in day-to-day merchandising, buying and restocking, supervising staff, serving customers, banking receipts, and paying bills, it is not difficult to lose track of the contribution per sale and in doing so, the bottom line.

A day-by-day comparison of gross profit contribution per sale with TARI, together with a comparison of the cumulative number of sales against target, kept the jeweler focused and motivated (Table 8-4).

Improving Profit

Table 8-4. Performance Summary Ending Week Ending _____

Day	Sales ($) A	Cost of Purchases ($) B	Gross Profit ($) C = (A − B)	Gross Profit (%) D = (C ÷ A)	Number of Sales E	Average Gross Profit per Sale($) F =(C ÷ E)
1	2,000	1,200	800	40	65	12.31
2	1,750	1,000	750	43	50	15.00
3	1,155	700	455	39	33	13.78
4	1,085	650	435	40	35	12.43
5	1,800	1,050	750	42	45	16.67
Total	7,790	4,600	3,190	41	228	13.99
Total b/f	47,000	27,000	20,000	42.5	1,425	14.04
Total c/f	54,790	31,600	23,190	42.3	1,653	14.03
Target	50,000	30,000	20,000	40	1,500	13.33
Variance	+4,790	+1,600	+3,190	+2.3	+153	+0.70

The effect of failing to complete a record such as Table 8-4 was driven home when reviewing client financial statements as part of a one-day workshop with some 20 clients.

One of the clients was the proprietor of an upmarket ladies' boutique. Her financial statement indicated no gross profit contribution at all. In other words sales equaled purchases; there was nothing left over to cover expenses, let alone make a profit.

"How did this come about?" I asked her.

"I don't really know," she replied. "It was my first year in business and I wanted to make a name for quality and service at reasonable prices."

"Were you discounting a lot?" I queried.

"Oh yes, it's a necessity in the boutique business."

"How much did you mark down when you discounted?"

"Fifty percent mostly," she said with a naïve smile.

"And how much did you markup purchases?"

"One hundred percent on average, I suppose"

I wrote down the data shown in Table 8-5:

Table 8-5. Analysis of Discounted Sale

A	Purchased Item at Cost	$100
B	Markup %	100%
C = (A × B)	Sale Price	$200
D	Discount %	50%
E = (C × D)	New Sale Price	$100

She blushed a deep red.

Later in the day, I spoke to the accountant about her problem. He said he had given her some advice about which books to keep when she started. But in his view, she couldn't afford to pay for more than the mandatory annual tax return, so he left her alone.

"Well, now she knows what her problem was," I said. "She should do better going forward."

This brings us to a real-life case study of a small business that drives home the importance of maintaining focus on the levers of activity and contribution.

CHAPTER

9

Upmarket Café Learns How to Stay on Track

Two friends in the hospitality industry open a café in an upmarket suburb and hit problems on the opening day. Fortunately, they had a wise mentor

---

The day arrived for opening. Jane and Ruth had combined forces to prepare for this day, when their new café would open its doors. Everything was brand new, from the café building itself to the tables, chairs, cutlery, crockery, and sparkling kitchen, replete with the latest equipment and a shining extraction flue over a gleaming white cooking range and oven.

They had prepared the menu very carefully. Their café was to be smart and casual in line with the suburb's upmarket image. And the menu had to fit the image—gourmet but not exclusively so, with prices pitched to match the type of customer they hoped to attract.

In addition to their combined experience as executive chef and assistant manager of a major city hotel, they were particularly fortunate to have a CPA friend, skilled in contribution-based activity analysis, who had insisted they prepare a financial projection of their expectations.

Following discussions with wholesale food and beverage suppliers, they made a careful research of similar cafés in the city and suburbs to gain an idea of the average price per serving.

They decided to plan for an average sale of $10; this would leave them an average gross profit contribution per sale of $7 after paying $3, or 30% of the $10, for the cost of food and beverage supplies (Table 9-1). Note that these were averages; someone spending $20 for lunch is balanced by another buying a cup of coffee to go.

Table 9-1. Targeting Average Contribution per Cover[1]

A	Target Average Sale	$10
B = (A × 30%)	Target Cost of Supplies	$3
C = (A − B)	Target Average Contribution	$7

Their next step was to work out how many sales or covers they would need in order to meet their expenses and make a profit.

Apart from rent, which was a known amount, the balance of expenses such as wages, leasing, insurance, repairs and maintenance, replacement of breakages, electricity, phones, and so forth, were guesstimates that would need adjustment as the picture became clearer down the track.

Having ignored a full wage for themselves in expenses, they now took account of their own needs, as well as including a 25% return on the overall investment of $140,000 (Table 9-2).

Table 9-2. Targeting the Annual Number of Covers

A	Target Expenses	$125,000
B	Target Profit	$85,000
C = (A + B)	Target Contribution	$210,000
D = TARI	Target Average Contribution (TARI)[2]	$7
E = (C ÷ D)	Target Covers	30,000

---

[1] A sale in a café/restaurant is known as a "cover."
[2] The target average contribution of $7 was a benchmark against which the average contribution of a sale could be measured. It was named "target average rate index," or TARI, to emphasize its benchmark status.

"They were a bit put off when they saw they would need 30,000 servings to achieve target. It gave them some sleepless nights," their CPA mentor informed me later. "But when we broke it down into daily bites, they began to relax."[3]

Their next step was to decide how many of the year's 365 days the café would open for business. What did the other cafés do? Did they open on public holidays, Sundays, Easter, and Christmas? When they thought about this, they realized they didn't really know.

More days of market research was undertaken before they decided the café would open for 338 days. They targeted an average daily contribution accordingly (Table 9-3).

Table 9-3. Targeting Daily Average Contribution

A	Target Covers	30,000
B	Days Open	338
C = (A ÷ B)	Target Average Covers per Day	89
D = (TARI)	Target Average Contribution (TARI)	$7
E = (C × D)	Target Average Daily Contribution	$623

The opening day brought a touch of mayhem. Over 150 customers were served, one part-time employee failed to turn up, the health inspector condemned the flue over the stove, and the dishwasher overflowed across the kitchen floor.

As if that were not enough, even though the total contribution for the day was well above expectations because of the numbers, they found the average contribution per cover was $6.13 compared with the TARI of $7.

Concluding that this was mainly due to the sale of menu items at the lower end of the scale and determined to get closer to their TARI of $7, they sat down at midnight and rewrote the menu.

Failing to reach the $7 target the next day, they again stayed up late and rewrote the menu, and again the third and the fourth nights until they got it right.

Eighteen months later, while enjoying a coffee in the café, I asked Ruth how things were working out. She told me they now employed six part-time staff

---

[3] The joint proprietors were not in a position to realize how fortunate they were to have such a mentor as their CPA friend. Without his wise guidance, they would have plunged in where angels fear to tread.

and had managed to get the cost of provisions down from 30% to 23% of sales by buying directly at the markets. They were still monitoring the average contribution and the number of covers daily and accumulatively as well as keeping a firm grip on expenses. She showed me some figures she'd been studying that proved she had a good grasp of what it takes to succeed in business (Table 9-4).

Table 9-4. Tracking Results Week Ending _____

Date	Sales($)	Gross Profit (%)	Gross Profit Contribution ($)	Number of Covers	Average per Cover($)
8/10	718	77	553	78	7.09
8/11	845	77	651	89	7.31
8/17	945	77	728	99	7.35
Total[4]	5,863	77	4,515	618	7.31
10 Weeks	61,418	77	47,292	6,478	7.30
Total c/f	67,281	77	51,807	7,097	7.00
11-Week Target	66,749	77	51,397	7,342	7.00
Variance	+532		+410	–245	+0.00

Case Comment

While serving gourmet food and brewing top-grade coffee was fundamental to the success of this business, the difference from the norm was that the proprietors knew the financial outcome they wanted, and what was needed to attain it.

Targeting a net profit of $85,000 on top of all expenses to achieve an annual gross profit of $210,000, and breaking it down across an estimated number of units (covers) into a target contribution per cover, is the easy part of the exercise.

The real difficulty is the follow-through.[5] Not many show the determination of these two proprietors, who were prepared to sit down after a tiring day and make it happen.

---

[4]Total covers 7 days—not just the 3 days listed here.
[5]As I mentioned in Chapter 5, a well-accepted adage in management consulting is that "genius is 20%, implementation 80%." In other words, there are many brilliant ideas, but the battle is only won in following through with the daily discipline of making them happen.

Sustaining the connection between a cash ring-up and the bottom line calls for a disciplined and ongoing commitment. Occasions will arise when the value and the point of the exercise will be questioned. It is then we need to be reminded of the underlying principle at work.

What exactly is this principle? It was a question that plagued me in my early days of working with numerous businesses across the country. To know it worked was one thing, but why?

The following real-life case study helped me resolve the "why?"

CHAPTER 10

Diesel Repair Shop Rescued from Sand-Up-Hill Country

A top sales engineer deciding on a change of lifestyle takes over a diesel repair business. As the business heads into liquidation, his wife discovers the way out

After two days' conducting workshops for 40 business clients of an accounting practice, I was ready to fly home, when John, one of the partners, said, "There's one client I really wanted to attend the workshop. He needs it more than any of the others, but he refused on the grounds he was too flat-out."

Chapter 10 | Diesel Repair Shop Rescued from Sand-Up-Hill Country

The accountant sighed, then said, "Fact is, he is heading down the tubes faster than a rabbit down a burrow and needs help badly. When his wife rang to apologize, I told her if she could get him into the office at 7:00 a.m., I would try to persuade you to stay another night."

He went on to tell me the client and his wife had sold their city home two years prior to buying a diesel repair business with a three-bedroom home and a few acres of land attached, mortgaging themselves heavily in the process.

The husband had been a sales engineer with a major company in the city, but he loved to get his hands dirty playing with diesel engines. Unless a miracle occurred, it looked like they would be bankrupt within a matter of weeks.

"Hmm," I said. "Sounds as though he's in sand-up-hill country." Although trying to sleep in a motel room fronting a noisy highway was no inducement, I agreed to stay the extra night.

In the morning, I headed for the conference room at John's office and found the couple already seated at the table, the wife making small talk with John. It was obvious from the outset the husband was not interested in advice from a so-called expert and resented being there.

In his mind, the solution to their financial problems lay back in the workshop fixing up diesel engines of trucks and fishing boats. That is where the action was, and that is where the money was to be made if they were to have any chance at all at clawing back their debt-ridden business.

His wife smiled an apology for him, as he sat hunched over the table, head in hands.

"How busy are you?" I asked.

She said, "We are very busy."

"Leaving out the cost of parts, what do you charge for an hour's work?"

"Thirty dollars," she said.

"How many hours are you open for work in the average week?"

"Oh, I don't know exactly," she replied, "but he works very long hours."

"Well let's say 60 hours a week, or 3,000 hours a year," I ventured.

"He works day and night and all weekends" she said, nudging him to respond. He emitted a faint groan.

I wrote on a sheet of paper in front of them:

$$3{,}000 \text{ hours} \times \$30 = \$90{,}000$$

"Did you get anything like this last year?"

"Oh no!" she exclaimed. "Nothing like that."

Improving Profit

"You actually billed $42,000," said John, looking at the accounts. "$12,000 for the cost of parts and $30,000 for labor."

"We certainly didn't!" she said adamantly.

"Well, you did bill $42,000. You were paid $22,000 and the balance of $20,000 is in accounts receivable," said John.

"Accounts receivable?" she queried. "Do you mean farmers?" referring to the great majority of their customers.

"If you billed $30,000 for labor, and worked 3,000 hours, either you must have charged closer to $10 an hour, or some 2,000 hours were not billed," I said.

"No," she replied. "I do all the billing, and we never charge less than $30 an hour."

"In that case, you charged out only 1,000 hours to bill $30,000—or roughly 20 hours a week. You must have many interruptions?" I quietly suggested.

"Oh yes, the phone never stops," she said.

"Don't you take messages?"

"Yes, but they're all urgent and they want to talk to him right away."

I wrote PHONE on a sheet.

"Any other interruptions?"

"Oh yes, the farmers," she said.

"What about the farmers?" I asked.

"Well, they walk straight into the workshop and start talking. Maybe they want an exhaust pipe welded or something. He has to stop what he is doing and attend to them and afterwards they say, 'How much?' and he says, 'A couple of dollars' and they say, 'Put it on the account.'

"And farmers do talk slowly," she added as an afterthought.

I wrote FARMERS on the sheet.

"Anything else?"

"Well, there's the garage mechanics," she said.

"What about them?"

"They come straight into the workshop and ask for advice."

"Why do they do that?"

"Well, he's a top diesel man, the best in the region. He can pick a problem in an engine as the truck comes up the hill to the workshop, just by listening to it."

Chapter 10 | Diesel Repair Shop Rescued from Sand-Up-Hill Country

She looked at her husband with a touch of pride. Hunched over the table, he was silently shaking his head, anxious to be back in sand-up-hill country.

"Do you mean he can do the work in half the time of the average mechanic?" I asked.

"A quarter," she said.

"In that case," I replied, "he could charge $60 an hour and still be cheaper than the average mechanic."

"Bullshit!" rang through the air like a shotgun, expressing pent-up disgust and disagreement over what was taking place, as though to suggest that if he charged $60 an hour he would be laughed out of business overnight.

Seeking a solution to what seemed to be a hopeless situation, I addressed the wife.

"Do you think that if the interruptions could be fixed, such as putting netting around the workshop to force farmers and garage mechanics through the office entrance, and getting customers to realize he will take messages and ring them back after say, 4:00 p.m., that you could extract 7 billable hours a day?" I asked.

"If you could do that for a 5-day week, plus say 5 hours on Saturday, it would mean 40 billable hours. And if you upped the $30 to $40, that would bring in $1,600 a week or close to $80,000 a year from hours charged."

She nodded somewhat uncertainly. "If something could be done about the interruptions, I suppose we could."

I went to the whiteboard and laid out the plan (Table 10-1).

Table 10-1. Projecting Annual Contribution

A	Target Billable Units per Week	40 hours
B	Target Average Contribution (TARI)	$40
C = (A × B)	Target Average Weekly Contribution	$1,600
D	Target Number of Weeks	48
E = (C × D)	Target Annual Contribution	$76,800

She smiled, and I wasn't sure whether she was merely being polite or maybe glimpsing a possible means of escape from a situation that was threatening the demise of what had once been a happy family unit.

Improving Profit

We used an Action Sheet (Table 10-2) to spell out who was to do what. She agreed to accept responsibility for extracting the 40 hours and billing at average contribution rate of $40 a week plus the cost of parts. John elected to help by getting the accounts receivables collected and arranging for netting to be placed around the workshop.

Table 10-2. Action Sheet

Date	Item	Action	Who	When
9/9	Billable Hours	Ensure 40 billable hours a week by an average of $40 contribution per hour + cost of parts	Mary	9/9
9/9	Phone Calls	Alert customers to new phone arrangements	Mary	9/10
9/9	Workshop	Secure workshop from direct entry	John	9/10
9/9	Account Receivable	Outstanding accounts to be followed up	John	9/10
9/9	Review	Meet to review progress	Mary/John	9/30

Present at meeting: MS, BS, JG, KC

Saying goodbye to John later, I expressed a sense of my inadequacy concerning the interview. The wife in particular, I felt, was expecting a lot more from the visiting "expert."

A few months later, I bumped into John at a conference. "How are they going?" I asked.

"Keeping their noses in front. The simple formula seems to be working," said John with a smile.

About 18 months later, John told me they were out of their troubles and going well.

"By the way," he asked, "what did you mean when you told me he was in sand-up-hill country?"

I said, "That's the place where you shovel all day with a shovel full of holes. It's not very productive, but you do go home feeling something good must have happened, because you are exhausted from a hard day's work."

"Oh, I see." said John. "Sounds like a typical tax practice to me."

Case Comment

Because this particular interview took place very early in my outreach to business, some time passed before I came to understand and grasp the importance of what had transpired.

In reviewing the interview, I recalled the target set for the wife was a weekly one. That was a little unusual bearing in mind that at the time, I only thought in terms of monthly feedback.[1]

I think it was because I couldn't imagine her informing her husband on the last day of the month, probably around midnight as he eased his tired body between the sheets, that he had only completed 140 hours this month and would need to do 180 next month to catch up.

Apart from the unlikelihood of catching up on a 20-hour backlog, I could only guess his response to such an approach. However, there was a good chance of catching up on a week's deficit of, say, 4 hours.

Weekly feedback was obviously important and that would have played a part in their recovery, although that in itself was not an adequate explanation for the turnaround. There was something more, and it only occurred to me some months later.

In addition to ordering parts, preparing invoices, chasing debtors, handling demands of the bank and suppliers, coping with phone calls, and other numerous events in the day-to-day life of business, she was also chief cook and bottle washer, bed maker, and mother to two small children. She was doing everything she could as best as she could, and all the time fighting a growing sense of depression as she saw their life savings fading away with no light at the end of the tunnel.

The truth was that although every activity mattered in one way or another, she had no awareness of the key activity fundamental to their survival: 40 billable hours at $40 a week.

It was only when she focused on extracting 7 billable hours a day from her husband and invoicing them out at the rate of 40 hours a week plus cost of parts that the business began to get on track.

The term *Contribution-Based Activity* encapsulated the concept: the contribution being $40 and the activity 40 billable hours. Simple enough, yet so fundamentally important, as the garment manufacturer was to discover in the next chapter.

---

[1] Because I had been nurtured on traditional financial statements, the importance of weekly feedback did not really take root so easily. I had thought my push for more frequent feedback of quarterly and even monthly statements, comparing actual with budget, was a fairly advanced concept at the time!

CHAPTER 11

Garment Maker Multiplies Net Profit by 700%

Caught up in the traditional approach to pricing, the owner and sales manager are excited about applying the concepts opened up by CBA/TARI.

A partner of the accounting practice drove me to his client's clothing factory and introduced me to a smilingly alert owner and his attractive designer wife. After the formalities and a tour of the factory, we settled down in the conference room.

"How do you price your garments?" I asked.

"Well, we go to the larger retail outlets and check the selling price of say, a pair of shorts, then we'll come back and work out how much we can make them for in addition to making a profit for us as well as the retailer."

The owner put several costing sheets on the table. Each listed the garments made, the material type and size, along with the type of accessories, such as buttons, zippers, cotton thread, buckles, and so forth.

Chapter 11 | Garment Maker Multiplies Net Profit by 700%

A percentage was added to the cost of material and accessories, and a rate per minute was applied to the time. The result was known as "the cost," to which a 40% markup was then applied. Table 11-1 provides an example.

Table 11-1. Pricing One Garment

A	Cost of Materials and Accessories	$8.00
B	Time to Make—33.75 Minutes	
C	Rate per Minute—20 Cents	
D = (B × C)	Cost to Make	$6.75
E = (A + D)	Total Cost	$14.75
F = (F × 40%)	Markup 40%	$ 5.90
G = (F + E)	Garment Price	$20.65

"Why 40 percent markup?" I asked.

"That's to cover overhead and profit," he replied.

"And do you find the overhead and profit are being covered as the year progresses?" I queried.

"Well, not really, I guess. That's one of the reasons we are having this chat!"[1]

"How many are employed in making the garments?"

"We employ 30 people full time as well as subcontractors."

"What level of productivity are you getting from the in-house staff?"

"We have the completed garments tallied each day and know exactly how many minutes have been put into them. It works out to 7 hours and 44 minutes of an 8-hour day, or 93 percent," he said proudly."[2]

Ninety-three percent was surprising. I asked, "You're sure the estimated times for garments are not too generous?"

---

[1] Applying 40% markup to a garment is based on the assumption it will cover overhead and profit. Obviously, if the cost of garments is down due to less demand or cheaper materials, the 40% markup will only partially cover overhead and profit; thus the need for tracking weekly and accumulatively to compare actual results with target.

[2] It is interesting to note that the financial impact of the daily and accumulated tally of garment numbers in the factory will only be reflected in the monthly financial and management account summaries presented toward the middle of the following month to which the data refers. That makes it difficult to correct course in a timely fashion.

"No," he said. "We test the times across several mock-ups to work out the best way of handling the flow of work beforehand."

I continued. "It appears the subcontractors produce about two-thirds of the output at a rate of 20 cents a minute."

The accountant chimed in. "That's right—the 20 cents takes into account both in house and out of house production.

"I see," I said. "Let's see what the average gross profit contribution per minute was last year." I went to the whiteboard (Table 11-2).

Table 11-2. Establishing Contribution[3] per Unit (Minute)[4] for the Past Year

A	Sales	$6,000,000
B	Materials at Cost	$2,100,000
C = (A − B)	Gross Profit Contribution	$3,900,000[5]
D	Expenses	$3,800,000
E = (C − D)	Net Profit	$100,000
F	Number of Units	9,000,000
G = (C ÷ F)	Unit-Contribution	43.3 cents

After a moment, the accountant spoke. "Are you including the subcontractors as part of labor expense?"

"Yes," I replied.

"Why? Shouldn't you include the cost of subcontractors with the cost of materials?"

It was a good point; subcontractors would normally be ranked as suppliers to a business.

---

[3] *Contribution* refers to the amount left over from a sale after paying the supplier. Normally referred to as *gross profit* or *gross profit contribution*, it is used frequently throughout this book to emphasize the reality that a business is not in business to pay a supplier, but to cover its own expenses and make a profit.

[4] The two key drivers of any business relate to billed units of activity multiplied by the average contribution per unit. A unit in this business—garment making—refers to a minute of time. Thus a reference to unit-contribution refers to the contribution per minute. In retailing, by contrast, a unit will refer to a sale or cash ring-up; in manufacturing and service, a unit will normally refer to a production- or machine-hour.

[5] Includes the subcontractors at $1.2 million (6,000,000 minutes × 20 cents).

Chapter 11 | Garment Maker Multiplies Net Profit by 700%

"Normally I would agree with you," I replied. "But on this occasion, the subcontractors are supplying 6 million or two-thirds of the 9 million minutes driving output. At 20 cents a minute—or $12 an hour—they are being paid much the same wage as the in-house staff. Apart from that, I am presuming some of the garments you produce are made by a combination of in-house and out-of-house?"

The accountant's brow furrowed in thought as the owner nodded agreement.

I continued. "Let's see how 43 cents unit-contribution compares with the unit-contribution in a sample of the current range of garments," I suggested, drawing up columns on the whiteboard, as they made ready to call out the numbers for Table 11-3.

Table 11-3. Comparison of 43 Cents Unit-Contribution with the Unit-Contribution from a Sample of Garments

Garment Style No.	Invoice Price ($) A	Material Cost ($) B	Contribution ($) C = (A − B)	Contribution (%) D = (C ÷ A)	Number of Units (Minutes) E	Average per Unit (Cents) F = (C ÷ E)
114	12	5	7	58	25	28
119	14	6	8	57	27	30
126	19	8	11	58	27	41
132	18	6	12	67	20	60
144	16	9	7	44	27	26
153	15	7	8	53	32	25
167	30	12	18	60	26	70
175	33	14	19	58	34	56

"We'll take the cost of materials from the invoice sale price and divide the resulting contribution by the number of minutes to make. That will give us a fix on the unit-contribution for comparison with last year's unit-contribution average of 43 cents."

The owner scratched his head. "How come we have an overall average contribution of 43 cents a minute compared with a range of up to 70 cents in the sample?"

"Doesn't the 43 cents depend on the number of units sold in each style, so that if more are sold of, say, styles 144 and 153, the average will fall?" replied the accountant.

Improving Profit

We agreed it might be informative to multiply the number sold in each style by the minutes and calculate the total contribution per garment style rather than the contribution per single garment. However, given the software limitations, it would be a lengthy process. So we moved on to consider the significance of the variety of gross profit contributions per minute stemming from the different garments.

We called in the sales manager to take part in the discussion. He was especially intrigued by the range of numbers. Pointing to style number 167 and its contribution of $18 per garment, he asked, "Does that mean if I sell 1,000 units of 167, we get a gross profit contribution of $18,000?"

I nodded.

"If I'd known that last week," he continued, "I could have won an order for 1,000 of 167. As it is, we lost it because we could not get the price down enough to beat the competition."

"Why?" I asked.

"Our policy only allowed me to drop 10 percent, and I needed to drop 20 percent. But even with a 20 percent price reduction, we would still have made a gross profit contribution of $14,400."

He looked over at the owner. "Boss, this is great stuff!" he exclaimed. "It's going to make all the difference to our sales. Now I'll know what to push and what not to push."

Pointing to style number 114, with a contribution of $7, he asked, "If I sell a thousand of 114, we get a gross profit of $7,000, even though both have taken up much the same time to make?"

I assured him that was the case and explained that, as long as he kept the overall contribution target in view, to which all styles contributed, they would stay on track. The key for an increased bottom line was to push the styles with the higher contribution and work out ways and means of raising the unit contribution from the lower contributors by better buying of materials or more efficient processes.

With that, we agreed to project an increased net profit for the year ahead, upping the target average unit-contribution from 43 cents to 48 cents. I explained that we would refer to the 48 cents as the target average rate index—TARI—a benchmark against which the contribution per minute from the various styles would be compared, quote by quote or invoice by invoice.

"But," the accountant said, "our expenses will no doubt rise next year. Even with a contribution of 48 cents, maybe we won't improve profit."

Chapter 11 | Garment Maker Multiplies Net Profit by 700%

"Good point," I said. "Let's take a closer look." We ran through all the expense items from the previous year. Maintaining staff numbers at the same level, we ended up increasing last year's $3,800,000 in expenses by 5 percent to $3,990,000.

We also assumed we could maintain in-house productivity at 93% and produce the same output of 9 million units as per the previous year. Table 11-4 shows the target plan.

Table 11-4. Targeting Performance Based on Increasing Unit-Contribution

A	Target Number of Units (Minutes)	9,000,000
B	Target Average Rate (TARI)	$0.48
C = (A × B)	Target Contribution	$4,320,000
D	Target Expenses	$3,990,000
E = (C − D)	Net Profit	$330,000

"That's a $230,000 increase on last year's net profit of $100,000. It's a bit optimistic, don't you think?" the owner queried.

"I reckon we can get it," said the sales manager, smiling enthusiastically. "Now that I know where we are going, we can soon work out what we need to sell to get there."

"Just for fun," said the owner, "let's see what kind of sales we'd need if we remain stuck at the same 43 cents." I sketched out what unit activity, measured in number of minutes, would be required to achieve the same net profit at last year's unit contribution of 43 cents. (Table 11-5)

Table 11-5. Targeting Unit-Activity to Achieve $330,000 Net Profit

A	Target Net Profit	$330,000
B	Target Expenses	$4,390,900[6]
C = (A × B)	Target Contribution	$4,720,000
D	Target Unit Contribution	$0.43
E = (C ÷ D)	Target Units	11,000,000[7]

---

[6]Outsourcing an additional 2 million units at 20 cents each boosted expenses by an additional $400,000.
[7]Rounded up from 10,976,674 units.

Improving Profit

Remaining at 43 cents per unit, and targeting the same net profit as in Table 11-3, called for close to an additional 2 million units to achieve the same outcome.

"I'm shocked," said the owner.

"Yes," I said. "It really drives home the importance of the two levers—activity and contribution. If you can't get one to move, try the other. But in this case it looks far more likely that you'd be able to get the 48 cents' contribution than having to increase output by a couple of million minutes."

I explained the key to success was to capture invoiced sales, contribution, and unit output, weekly and accumulatively, and then compare them to the target.[8]

"How," asked the owner, "might we get from 43 cents to 48?"

I said, "You have several options at your disposal:

- "Push for more sales of those garments contributing more than 43 cents,
- "Review times to make garments contributing less than 43 cents, or
- "Review material supplies to reduce buying price where possible."

During the ensuing three years, the firm went on to treble sales to $18 million, boosting net profit to $1 million, and using the funds to build a state-of-the-art factory containing the very latest technology coupled with outstanding working conditions for the employees.

It was then that import duty was reduced to the point where cheaply produced garments from overseas created such pressure on prices that, had the proprietors lacked a clear idea of where to direct their energies, they would have gone under. As it was, in order to sustain profitable growth, they subcontracted offshore.

Case Comment

Seven new and important aspects of this business were highlighted in this case:

- Identifying the average gross profit per unit (minute) as an important step on the way to improve profitability. The point: it is not possible to improve on an unknown.

---

[8]Table 1-2 (Chapter 1) illustrates a simple format for tracking weekly results for comparison with target.

- The range in contributions per unit of different styles.
- The potential of accurate contribution information in helping the sales manager make spot decisions on pricing and winning new sales.
- The importance of comparing weekly and long-term actual contribution with target contribution, based on unit activity × unit contribution.
- The folly of inflexible discount policies that inhibit sales and contribution.
- The feasibility of targeting an increase of 5 cents per minute from 43 to 48 cents.
- The clarity achieved by separating the cost of materials from the contribution necessary to cover operating expenses plus profit.

The contribution per unit per style of garment in Table 11-3 came as a surprise to a management steeped in a traditional approach to costing and pricing based on percentage markups on materials and labor prior to adding a further 40% markup to cover overhead and profit. The approach masks the contribution per unit of activity—in this case a minute of time. In doing so, it obscured an important decision-making tool.

In the next chapter, you'll find a real-life case study that reinforces the methodology underlying invoice analysis. It explains how gross profit contribution per key unit of activity is obtained from the analysis, and how that information can be used to pinpoint the actual level of activity (productivity) in a business.

CHAPTER 12

Switchboard Manufacturer Climbs into the Black

While senior management held conflicting views about the cause of declining profitability, a representative sample of invoices helped pinpoint the problem in a matter of minutes

Financial statements—emerging four months after the end of the financial year—only confirmed what was already known: the business was losing ground and fast.

The cause of the decline was hard to pinpoint. Everybody in the place, ranging from the CEO to the office assistant, seemed to have a different point of view.

Chapter 12 | Switchboard Manufacturer Climbs into the Black

The production manager put the problem down to the new computer system installed at great expense 18 months earlier. The consultant that sold the deal as being the latest and the best on the market was still working on it. The software pumped out information by the ream, but the detail was so extensive that it masked a clear view.

The marketing manager felt the problem lay in production, which, ever since the new computer system was installed, hadn't kept time sheets. As he saw it, there seemed to be no control over employee hours anymore, resulting in quotes that had become increasingly uncompetitive.

The accountant was of the opinion the new system was really quite effective because it could give any variety of report. The problem, in his view, was that the consultant had yet to complete certain adjustments. As a result, he was unable to extract relevant information about contractual commitments. He agreed the loss was serious, but in his view it lay outside his area of responsibility. He believed the problem was most likely due to a declining economic environment.

I happened to be in the accountant's office when one of the company's sales representatives walked in to discuss a potential order. Following an exchange of formalities, I asked him how he worked out the price for a job.

"I have a price list for the parts and the costing section works out the hours needed to set up and install the system," he replied.

"Do you compare the quoted times with the actual times?" I asked the accountant.

"Not really," he replied. "The production manager says the work is carried out as quickly and efficiently as it can be done, so he doesn't take any notice of the quoted times, although he does input the completed times."

"And the system doesn't carry out a check of actual times with quoted times?"

"Not yet. The consultants say they are working on it."

My discussions with the owner revealed a different perspective from that of the accountant. He said the business was needed a new plant and equipment if it was to remain competitive, but that called for capital injection. Given the state of the company's accounts, the bank had severely restricted all credit facilities.

I reviewed all the financial reports provided and noted that they summarized results in traditional management-accounting format, complete with variances from budget for labor, Materials, and expenses. Even with interpretation, the reports lacked relevance to the pressing needs of management for a forest-level view.

The previous year's financials revealed that a gross profit contribution of $5 million, calculated as sales less cost of materials, failed to cover expenses, resulting in a net loss of $200,000.

I asked for a representative sample of invoices that would list the sales price, the cost of purchases, and preferably the quoted rather than the time-sheet hours (Table 12-1).[1]

Table 12-1. Invoice Analysis Identifying Average Contribution per Production-Hour Unit

Job Number	Sale Price ($) A	Cost of Purchases ($) B	Contribution ($) C= (A − B)	Contribution (%) D= (C ÷ A)	Units (Hours) E	Average per Unit ($) F= (C ÷ E)
345	3,600	1,750	1,850	51	4.84	382
348	2,200	660	1,540	70	12	128
351	2,000	1,536	464	23	7	66
356	960	90	870	91	5.8	150
360	1,900	310	1,590	84	13	122
362	2,050	396	1,654	81	8.8	188
Total	12,710	4,742	7,968	63	51.4	155

The analysis revealed an average gross profit contribution per unit-hour of $155.

Dividing the total contribution of $5 million by $155 per hour provided a close guesstimate of hours charged out for the period (Table 12-2).

Table 12-2. Identifying Productivity

A	Total Contribution	$5,000,000
B	Average Unit Contribution	$155
C = (A ÷ B)	Hours Billed	32,258
D	Hours Available	65,000
E = (C ÷ D × 100)	Productivity	50%

---

[1] Quoted hours are invariably less than time-sheet hours. See chapter 5 for an example of what tends to happen with time-sheet hours.

Chapter 12 | Switchboard Manufacturer Climbs into the Black

The CEO looked shocked that at 50% productivity, the company was billing for only four hours of labor each eight-hour day. The marketing manager nodded agreement, the production manager frowned in disbelief, and the accountant queried the reliability of the invoice sample.

I pointed out that regardless of the reliability of the sample, there was little to be gained by spending time and money delving into historical records. The true situation would be revealed over the next few weeks as we tracked actual results against target.

It was time to plan ahead by projecting expenses, adding the desired net profit and targeting an increase in productive hours from four to five hours per eight-hour day (Table 12-3).

Table 12-3. Planning Ahead and Targeting the Plan

A	Expenses (Excluding Materials)	$5,200,000
B	Target Net Profit	$300,000
C = (A + B)	Target Gross Profit	$5,500,000
D	Paid Production Hours	65,000
E = (D × 62.5%)	Target Chargeable Hours Based on Achieving 5 hours per 8-Hour Day or 62.5% of Paid Hours	40,625
F = (C ÷ E)	Target Average Contribution per Hour	$135
G = (C ÷ 45 weeks)	Average Weekly Gross Profit Target	$122,222
H = (E ÷ 45 weeks)	Average Weekly Hours	903 hours

Because of the targeted increase in chargeable hours, the target average unit-contribution—referred to as the target average rate index or TARI[2]—of $135, was $20 under the average gross profit per hour of $155 from the invoice sample.

This led to heated debate about which benchmark should be adopted: $135 or $155?

I pointed out that it would be unwise to track against a benchmark lower than the one showing up in the sample. To put their minds at ease, we analyzed an additional sample of 20 invoices and confirmed the initial sample by coming up with $155.

---

[2] So named to identify its status as a benchmark or index; not to be confused with "cost."

Using $155 and improving productivity from four to five hours a day would provide an additional contribution of $800,000, boosting overall contribution from $5,200,000 to $6,300,000.

"I don't see how we are going to get the work," said the CEO, to a chorus of agreement.

"Why don't we just start and see what happens?" I suggested, knowing from experience that once they started tracking quotes against the TARI benchmark of $155 and an average weekly target of 905 hours, they would achieve the competitive advantage necessary to secure additional work—subject of course to getting the supervisor and other key players on their side, a process that called for weekly action meetings.[3]

It was time to introduce the Action Sheet, without which nothing of consequence would happen (Table 12-4).

Table 12-4. Action Sheet

Date	Item	Action	Who	When
03/12	Quotes	Compare quotes with TARI	MM	3/12
03/12	Time Sheets	Compare quotes with time-sheets on completion	PM, MM	3/12
03/12	Feedback	Complete invoice analysis weekly and accumulatively	AC	3/19
03/12	Next Meeting	8:00 a.m.	CEO, MM, PM, FD	3/19

Present at meeting: CEO, MM, PM, AC, KC

Tracking invoiced sales, gross profit, and hourly rates weekly and accumulatively slowly but surely brought the business back on track.[4]

Quotations were compared with the TARI benchmark for the contribution rate per unit-hour before they were sent out and again before they were committed to production. The managers closely examined rates that showed less than $155 to see if (a) the hours could be reduced by examining ways and means of improving efficiency or (b) the cost of purchases could be reduced.

By the end of six months, the company started to earn a profit and by year's end, profit was close to $350,000, or $50,000 in excess of the 12-month target.

---

[3]For more on the role of action meetings, see Chapter 22.
[4]Table 1-2 illustrates a simple format for tracking weekly results for comparison with target.

Asked what they put the improvement down to, the CEO gave the following reasons:

- Confidence when they quote because they can compare hourly quote rates with TARI
- Speed, because they get weekly as well as accumulative results each Friday after closing the books on Wednesday

Knowing the bottom line when quoting puts them well ahead of their competitors.

Case Comment

The company appeared to be a busy enterprise that manufactured specialized switchboards for sale as well as contracting to install, repair, and maintain them.

The receptionist gave a strong impression of efficiency; the corridors leading to the offices were brightly painted and the floor tiles gleamed from their early morning polish.

The offices were equally impressive, as was the welcome from the CEO and line management. At that first meeting, there were no overt signs of a dysfunctional management pulling in different directions. That only became apparent during individual interviews.

The fact that each of the line managers had a different view as to why the company was unprofitable was a clear indication of poor cohesion, inevitably leading to a lack of direction and focus.

There was a sense that the new software being installed would provide all the answers. But as is so often the case, without cohesive input by the key players, new software only serves to exacerbate rather than eradicate an existing weakness.

In any event, the software, programmed to deliver feedback according to accepted accounting methodology, albeit more expeditiously than its forerunner, was already proving to be a problem by virtue of the sheer volume of output.

The accountant tacitly accepted a situation in which quoted times for jobs were never matched with actual times in the time sheets because the production manager had no confidence in the quoted times. This was not atypical of manufacturing businesses, where output is dependent on the production manager, who becomes highly dependent on his subordinate engineers as years pass and he fails to keep up with the latest technology.

The invoice analysis brought a touch of reality, as management viewed the range of unit-contributions and came to realize the level to which productivity had fallen. With confidence shaken, it was timely to plan ahead and develop a target.

While acknowledging the feasibility of improving productivity from four to five billable hours per eight-hour day, they were tentative about the likely level of demand for the increased output.

Without weekly meetings and action assigned to whom and by when on an Action Sheet, there was no way they would have brought off such a successful turnaround. Knowing it would be fatal to walk away and leave them to complete the Action Sheet, I arranged to be at the first four meetings, following which I had the secretary e-mail copies weekly.[5]

Step by step, as line managers began to get weekly feedback[6] and could see the impact of their decisions, they began to cohere and operate as a team.

The growing recognition of interdependence brought a deeper appreciation of one another's roles and the problems encountered. For example, armed with a newfound understanding of contribution as distinct from sales, marketing initially discounted sales with a unit-contribution[7] in excess of $155.

This in turn put more pressure on production, pushing the plant into overtime, increasing wages, and lowering the overall average unit-contribution.

The weekly action meeting brought these matters and other problems into the light and became instrumental in resolving them. The company moved forward as a result.

Businesses dependent on production output tend to defer to the production manager, often to the detriment of the bottom line. The impact of this becomes more apparent in the next chapter.

---

[5]Chapter 22 provides examples of the quiet yet persistent pressure of the Action Sheet on participants to complete a task they have agreed to undertake.
[6]The accountant had arranged for weekly and accumulative analysis of invoices to compare the actual unit-contribution with TARI.
[7]A unit in this case being a billable production- or man-hour.

CHAPTER 13

Baker Identifies Where the Rubber Meets the Road

Immersed in baking and distributing 750 products from meat pies to crumpets, it came as a shock when management caught a glimpse of the woods from down in the trees.

The management committee, composed of department heads, sat around the boardroom table. The CEO had called them together at 10 minutes' notice to hear what I had to say, and it was apparent they resented the short notice.

He invited me to speak freely and openly about my findings to date. As I had been walking around and speaking with a variety of managers and supervisors for the past two days, I had already met most of them. But the gray-haired lady closeted in a back office, from whom I had gathered the details resulting in the information I was about to use, was not among them.

"I have taken a look at the range of 750 products, and I'd like to demonstrate a technique which identifies potential winners and losers and gives a clear message to marketing and production in the process." I looked around the table to gauge interest.

"To start with, perhaps you could give me some idea of what you consider to be your most profitable product?" I asked.

"Crumpets" was the unhesitating and almost universal response. It was understandable; the winter season was in full swing and crumpets sold well in cold weather. They were a comparatively cheap food to produce, being little more than a light flour mixture pitted with holes and passed over a gas heater at the rate of 12,000 an hour.

"And the next most profitable?" I asked

Answers varied, ranging from meat pies, lemon tarts, and sandwich cake to sausage rolls.

"Well, ignoring the quantities sold for the moment and looking purely at the gross profit contribution per production man-hour, sausage rolls make the largest contribution at $250 per man-hour, followed by meat pies at $200, crumpets at $77, with sandwich cake as low as $25."

They sat and stared in stunned silence as I wrote the amounts on the whiteboard.

"How did you arrive at that information?" the CEO asked.

"The costing lady had all the information about the man-hours required to achieve each product as well as the cost of ingredients. It was a matter of getting a simple program written to extract the cost of ingredients, and dividing the resulting contribution by the number of hours involved. The result was gross profit contribution per man-hour."

"I'm sorry, but I still don't quite understand," said the CEO

I responded, "Well let's look at meat pies. A pie wholesales at 68 cents and the ingredients cost 18 cents, leaving a contribution of 50 cents. The plant churns out 10,000 an hour, which makes for a contribution of $5,000 per hour. With 25 staff involved in hands-on production of pies, the contribution works out at $200 per man-hour." I wrote it out on the whiteboard (Table 13-1).

Table 13-1. Identifying Contribution[1] per Unit[2] for Meat Pies

A	Wholesale Price per Meat Pie	68 cents
B	Ingredient Price	18 cents
C = (A − B)	Contribution per Pie	50 cents
D	Batch Production per Hour	10,000 pies
E = (C × D)	Contribution per Batch-Hour	$5,000
F	Batch Production Personnel	25
G = (E ÷ F)	Contribution per Unit (Production-Hour)	$200

The CEO looked puzzled. "I think I can grasp that, but how could the crumpets' contribution be so low considering they use a lot less labor than meat pies?"

"I agree," the production manager said in a tone of annoyance. He had been experiencing difficulty holding back. "The fact is, the contribution on most of the products is much the same based on 70 percent markup on factory cost."

"What do you mean by factory cost?" I asked him.

"Ingredients, direct and indirect labor, supervision, power, depreciation on plant, repairs, and maintenance, rent, phones, and so on."

"And how do you apportion these costs to the various products?" I asked.

"Direct costs such as ingredients, power, and labor go to the product and the rest are spread in proportion to the direct labor. We also apply a small markup to make a factory profit." He looked around the table before adding, "And the factory has never failed to make a profit."

"You say 70 percent is applied to all factory costs to arrive at the selling price, yet the selling price is pretty well dictated by the market, isn't it?" I asked.

"Mostly it is," said the CEO, steeped in the traditional approach to costing and pricing.

The meeting adjourned for lunch, during which time we went down to the crumpet line and saw crumpets being packed by hand as they came off the line. "They used to be machine packed into four a pack, but when we went to

---

[1] *Contribution* refers to the amount left over after deducting the cost of purchases (in this case, ingredients) from the sale price.
[2] *Unit* refers to a production- or man-hour.

six a pack and then eight a pack to meet the competition, we had to use hand labor," said the foreman. "It's slowed us down quite a bit." The production manager looked stunned.

After lunch, to avoid getting lost in the detail of costing and pricing issues, I suggested we look at the matter from a different angle altogether and went to the whiteboard.

"The sales target for next year is $30 million. If we take out $10 million for ingredients and packaging, we are left with $20 million gross profit. You are planning on paying for 220,000 direct labor hours, and you are estimating that 75 percent of these hours, or 165,000, will be productive." I wrote it down on the whiteboard (Table 13-2) and divided $20 million by 165,000 hours to arrive at $121.

Table 13-2. Developing a Target Average Contribution per Unit[3]

A	Sales	$30,000,000
B	Cost of Ingredients	$10,000,000
C = (A − B)	Contribution	$20,000,000
D	Available Units (Hours)	220,000
E	Target Productivity	75%
F = (D × E)	Target Billable Units (Hours)	165,000
G = (C ÷ F)	Target Average per Unit	$121

"This means that we need an average gross profit contribution of $121 per hour. We call it *target average rate index*, or TARI, to emphasize it is a benchmark and not a cost. Do we agree?" I looked around the table to see if they were with me.

"I don't see the point," grunted the production manager. "Where do factory costs, direct or indirect, come into that?"

"Excluding ingredients and packaging, all operational costs plus the planned profit are included in the gross profit contribution of $20 million. The $121 is the average contribution per hour based on 75 percent productivity. We need

---

[3] In this case, the "unit" of activity is a man-hour. There are numerous activities taking place in most businesses, but there is a key driving activity fundamental to the rest; in manufacturing, a unit of that activity will normally be a production-hour (whether by man or machine). In retailing it will be an invoiced sale or a cash ring-up.

to establish a simple program which will track the output hours as well as the contribution per hour. We should be in a position to summarize the data weekly and accumulatively and know where we are week to week compared with the plan."

"But what about the considerable variation in contribution from product to product that you pointed out?" asked the CEO.

"That's the very point of the exercise," I replied, pleased that he had raised the matter.

"With the TARI benchmark of $121, we are in a position to compare the actual contribution from any combination of the 750 active products and see if we can establish a direction for marketing or production or both."

I pointed to the whiteboard where I had listed the various contribution rates per production hour—rolls at $250, meat pies $200, crumpets $77, and sandwich cake $25. "Compared with a benchmark of $121 per hour, what are these figures telling us?" I asked.

"Flog sausage rolls and meat pies," said the marketing manager, sensing a possible removal of the shackles on pricing, which had held back marketing initiatives in the past.

"Boost efficiency in crumpets and get out of sandwich cake," the accountant offered.

The production manager had difficulty in restraining himself. "If you think you can get more efficiency in the crumpet line short of half a million on new plant, good luck to you."

Using an Action Sheet (Table 13-3), we agreed on who should do what by when and concluded the meeting.

Table 13-3. Action Sheet

Date	Item	Action	Who	When
8/9	Product Analysis	Check contribution rates	AC	8/9
8/9	Marketing	Prepare new marketing plan	MM	8/23
8/9	Crumpet Output	Report on how to improve	PM	8/16
8/9	Next Meeting		All	8/16

Present at Meeting: CEO, AC, PM. MM, KC

On a subsequent visit, I learned that the production manager had resigned to spend more time with his family. It was understandable. Overseeing an output of 750 products a day would drive most to an early retirement.

The finance manager had taken refuge in computer printouts, and the marketing manager, having won the battle to cull several low-selling products, pushed sausage rolls and meat pies and boosted profit to unprecedented levels. The CEO was pleased, but wondered why all this had not been explained before. It seemed so simple.

An interesting hangover from the traditional management-accounting reports surfaced a little further down the track. Based on the new production manager's belief that he could benefit from the available capacity and boost meat pie production with only a marginal increase in power costs, marketing made a deal—without seeking approval from the accountant—to sell meat pies to a supermarket chain at 50 cents, or 18 cents less than the normal wholesale price.

One Saturday morning, following a major promotional campaign, 120,000 pies sold, and the customers were still screaming for more when an ashen-faced production manager decided enough was enough, and threw the switch on a pastry-encrusted plant and a dough-splattered crew.

After deducting additional power and ingredient costs, the contribution to the bottom line from the exercise approximated $35,000.

However, the software, programmed to calculate discounts from the wholesale selling price of 68 cents, totaled a discount of $21,600 (Table 13-4), which in the traditional accounts presentation to the board of directors some weeks after the event, indicated that marketing had, in one hit, used up the budgeted discount for the whole year, leaving an ugly red deficit in the variance column.

Table 13-4. Bottom-Line Impact of Discounted Pies

A	Normal Wholesale Price per Pie	68 cents
B	Ingredient Cost per Pie	18 cents
C = (A − B)	Normal Contribution per Pie	50 cents
D	Discounted Price per Pie	50 cents
E	Ingredient Cost per Pie	18 cents
F = (D − E)	New Contribution per Pie	32 cents
G	Number of Pies Sold	120,000

Comparison of the net contribution of $35,000 with $36,300 (based on a TARI of $121 × 300 production-hours[4]) suggests the order was worth the effort, particularly when taking the favorable publicity into account.

However, from that time on, despite earnest attempts from marketing to explain the profitability of the exercise, there was a strict prohibition on repeating such an exercise—which, viewed philosophically, only serves to highlight the need to get the CEO on one's side beforehand.

Case Comment

Having established a TARI benchmark of $121 against which the contribution of each of 750 products could be measured, software was developed to extract the contribution from invoiced sales, for weekly and accumulative comparison.[5]

Sales reps were allocated an annual contribution target broken down to an average contribution per week, based on achieving an average contribution margin of 67%—the percentage relationship between $30 million sales and the $20 million contribution target (Table 13-5).

Table 13-5. Samples Analysis of Contribution per Representative

Rep	Sale ($) A	Ingredients at Cost ($) B	Contribution ($) C = (A − B)	Contribution Margin (%) D = (C ÷ A)	Units (Production Hours) E	Average per Unit ($)[6] F = (C ÷ E)
JJ	6,000	2,000	4,000	67	40	100
BK	4,500	1,500	3,000	67	25	120
LP	7,500	2,500	5,000	67	60	83
HD	5,700	1,900	3,800	67	42	90
Total	23,700	7,900	15,800	67	167	95

Table 13-5 illustrates a contribution margin of 67%, in line with the overall target contribution margin. On paper, the reps would appear to be on target.

However, the same analysis reveals an average unit rate of $95—a cause for concern should this become an ongoing trend. The sales manager would want to know what products BK is promoting compared with LP. It would be necessary to follow through on a weekly basis for the reps to grasp the need for pushing products exceeding the TARI of $121 per hour.

---

[4] Calculated from 25 persons to a shift times 12 hours at the rate of 10,000 pies an hour.
[5] Table 1-2 illustrates a simple format for tracking weekly results for comparison with target.
[6] "Unit" here refers to an hour of the representative's time.

Table 13-5 also highlights the benefit of measuring performance against TARI, in this case based on production-hours in addition to a desired contribution margin.

This business operated state-of-the-art software when it came to taking phone orders. Twenty-one phone receptionists keyed in orders received from school, factory, and office canteens, hotels, supermarkets, milk bars, cafés, delicatessens, and the like.

The software extracted the ingredients required for each order and accumulated a total ingredient quantity of flour, meat, sugar, butter, eggs, milk, and so forth, ready for the 7 p.m. arrival of bakers and pastry cooks.

As products streamed off the production lines, they were sorted and matched with orders, allocated into districts, and sent for dispatch to waiting delivery vehicles.

Without knowledge of the hours required per product, there was no simple way of identifying the level of productivity at which the plant operated.

Had it not been for the conscientious gray-haired costing clerk, hidden away in a small back office and neglected by all and sundry as a bygone relic, the information about costs of ingredients, packaging, and standard production times would not have been accessible without major expenditure of time and effort.

During one of my visits, a young, fresh-faced audit team from a major accounting firm proudly explained that their audit software was capable of identifying up to 96% confidence level in a sample audit check. They also pointed out a hardware box sitting on top of the computer mainframe. It was extracting selected data for a business intelligence system installed by the consulting arm of their firm as a means of providing management with various key performance indictors about the business.

Asked if they knew how the actual output compared with the potential output of the plant, they shrugged their shoulders. Asked if they knew how much waste product was dumped into a huge bin in the factory for removal twice a week, they had no idea. Neither item was on their audit checklist.[7]

---

[7]Although paid by the company, auditors check the accuracy and integrity of the financials on behalf of the company's shareholders and lenders. If they undertake management advice for the company they audit, they tread a fine line between the role of auditor and adviser, where conflicts of interest can and do arise—a conflict well portrayed in the rise and fall of Arthur Andersen. During an audit, although they are technically well placed to identify actual or potential problems and draw them to the attention of the company, their focus is strictly defined by the audit brief.

Nor, it seemed, was it on anyone's check list within the company. While the dump truck's collection of waste was known, the amount dumped was not. In the time available, I was unable to find out if there was a provision in the accounts for wastage.

Inquiries made of the dump truck operator revealed that 12 tons of waste product was dumped weekly. Composed mainly of strips of dough trimmed from long lines of pie pastry and sausage rolls, the amount was calculated to be worth close to $1 million, or 5% of total cost of ingredients. Whether the accounts provided for 5% of wastage of ingredients, I was unable to ascertain in the time available.

In the following chapter, we look at pricing as related to productivity through the eyes of a typical architectural practice.

CHAPTER 14

Architectural Practice Eradicates a Malignant Cancer

A variety of hourly charge rates based on salary levels, coupled with dysfunctional time sheets, were creating a major distraction until the partners were shown a new way.

Operating an upmarket architectural practice in the heart of the city, the partners of Smith and Co. were experiencing problems finding enough cash to pay wages and other expenses. They put this down to delays in sending out invoices for design and supervision work already carried out.

Believing the cause of the problem to be related to poor time-sheet control, they had gone out of their way to employ a strongly recommended clerical

Chapter 14 | Architectural Practice Eradicates a Malignant Cancer

assistant to ensure all time sheets were maintained correctly and on time. Despite all their efforts, daily completion of time sheets was still falling way behind.

Again and again, right in the middle of major design work, they had to put down their tools and spend valuable time checking work in progress in order to justify billing clients. In the eyes of the firm's partners, what was needed was an improved time-sheet system. They asked me if I would be able to help.

It didn't long to realize the time sheets were only a symptom of a deeper underlying problem.

Note The fees in an architectural practice are calculated in much the same way in professions such as accounting, legal, consulting engineering, surveying, and so forth, with rates reflecting various salary levels within the firm.

In the first instance, I asked for the target chargeable hours of the partners and staff with the various hourly charge rates. The chargeable hours were based on the industry average of 65% of paid hours. I did the analysis shown in Table 14-1.

Table 14-1. Identifying Potential Gross Fees

Position	Planned Chargeable Hours (65% of Paid Hours)	Hourly Charge Rate	Gross Fees
2 Partners	2,800	$250	$700,000
3 Senior Architects	3,200	$175	$560,000
2 Junior Architects	2,600	$80	$208,000
Technical Designers	3,600	$110	$396,000
Junior Technical Designers	2,600	$55	$143,000
Total	**14,800 hours**	**$136**	**$2,007,000**

The planned total charge-out times for partners and staff members amounted to 14,800 or 65% of paid hours. Multiplying the hours by the relevant hourly charge rates resulted in potential fees of $2,007,000.

Comparing potential fees with actual fees highlighted the real problem underlying the scarcity of cash (Table 14-2).

Table 14-2. Pinpointing Productivity

A	Potential Gross Fees	$2,007,000
B	Actual Gross Fees	$1,150,000
C = (B ÷ C)	Productivity	57% of target
D	Paid Hours	22,769
E = (D × 65%)	Chargeable Hours Targeted	14,800
F = (E × 57%)	Hours Actually Charged	8,436
G = (F ÷ D × 100)	Chargeable Hours to Paid Hours	37%

The fact that it took only a few minutes to demonstrate their productivity was running at a low level only exacerbated their discontent with the performance of the practice.

Rather than spend time looking back over somewhat fragmented and unreliable data, we agreed it would be more cost efficient to plan ahead and track results on a weekly basis. This would provide accurate information as well as highlight problem areas inhibiting progress.

I suggested they target an average fee of $142, which I referred to as a target average rate index, or TARI, to emphasize its statistical status. A TARI of $142 for an average weekly billing of 330 hours would ensure a gross revenue close to the annual target of $2,102,310 (Table 14-3).

Table 14-3. Planning and Targeting Performance

A	Total Expenses (including staff salaries)	$1,650,000
B	Target Net Profit (including partner salaries)	$450,000
C = A + B	Target Revenue (net of disbursements)	$2,100,000
D	Chargeable Hours	14,800 hours
E = (C ÷ D)	Target Average Hourly Rate	$142
G = (D ÷ 45 weeks)	Average Weekly Hours	329 hours
H = (E × G)	Average Weekly Billings	$46,718
I = (H × 45 weeks)	Check Annual Billing	$2,102,310

"Not sure we really understand what all that means," they said.

"It means that you are tracking an average of 330 hours by a TARI of $142 an hour weekly. It means that when you price your work in future, you divide the anticipated fees by a TARI of $142 to calculate the hours the job should take."

"But what if we use the juniors more than the seniors? The average rate will be much less than $142."

"It may, if you were able to track the individual hours that closely—which hasn't yet been possible despite all your efforts.

"On average, the $142 will be close to the mark. Assume you quote a fee of 10 percent of a $2,620,000 estimated construction cost. You divide your potential fee of $262,000 by $142 and work out that you need 1,845 hours. You project those hours over the various stages of design and supervision and commence monitoring the job weekly and accumulatively." I laid this all out on the whiteboard (Table 14-4).

Table 14-4. Example of Job Targeting

A	Quoted Construction Cost of Job 112	$2,620,000
B	Design and Supervision	10%
C = (A × B)	Target Fees	$262,000
D	TARI	$142
E = (C ÷ D)	Target Hours to Complete	1,845 hours

I suggested a weekly meeting of the key players would be necessary to review progress. At the meeting, they would need to review the hours spent on a job for comparison with the hours allocated. Where the times were in excess of expectations, they would estimate the time to complete. The meeting would serve to identify constraints and decide how to overcome them in order to meet target. It would also help them understand that watching the hours spent on a project and comparing it to the target was something that needed to become second nature for all in the firm. I laid out a scheme for tracking jobs (Table 14-5).

Table 14-5. Example of Job Tracking: Week Ending 7/11

Job	Target Hours	Hours to Date	Estimated Hours to Complete	Variance
112	1,845	945	1,000	−100
109	600	400	100	+100
99	3,000	2,500	700	−200

This in turn called for a daily collection of time-sheet hours, without which the firm would be back to square one. Recording times in a diary as one or two advocated would not ensure daily completion when times were freshly in mind.

I introduced the Action Sheet (Table 14-6) as a tried and tested way of getting the desired response. Knowing from experience it would take up to three weeks to bring about the changes, I arranged to attend the first three meetings to ensure the process grooved in correctly.

Table 14-6. Action Sheet

Date	Item	Action	Who	When
4/5	Time Sheets	Complete daily for collection	DK, MG, LS, BV, JK, SK	4/11
4/5	Job Update	Update actual times for comparison with allocated times	DK, MG, LS, BV, JK, SK	4/11
4/5	Billings	Prepare format to track billings for comparison with target, weekly and accumulatively	DK	4/11
4/5	Next Meeting		DK, MG, LS, BV, JK, SK	4/11

Present at meeting: DK, MG, LS, BV, JK, SK, KC

The meetings were attended by the two partners and four team leaders heading up the various jobs.

It took three weeks of sustained pressure by the partners to get the message through to staff that they needed to be serious about tracking hours before the process finally grooved in and control over billings was established.

As focus came to bear on the various jobs, hidden benefits emerged, such as a discussion of ways and means of reducing hours by varying the design to achieve greater efficiency and still maintain quality. The tone slowly but surely changed from one of laissez-faire or "she'll be right" to one of "how can we do this better?"

The firm overshot the annual target net profit by $75,000.

Case Comment

Architects are introduced to the calculation of fees during their university years. In essence, they are taught to work out a charge rate by multiplying the basic wage by a factor based on the relationship of wages to total revenue.

Thus, a practice with wages of $400,000 and budgeting for a $1 million in revenue would multiply each dollar of wage by 2.5. It means that a junior getting, say, $17 an hour would be budgeted to charge out at $42 an hour, while a senior getting $100 an hour would be charging $250.

This approach is common to similar professions and is based on a theoretical assumption that a fee charged to a client reflects the level of skill and experience involved. In other words, a junior charging $42 an hour will take roughly six times longer than the senior charging $250 an hour.

For a client paying the fee, it is of little consequence who did what as long as the job is completed satisfactorily and is in line with the quote. It is of no satisfaction to the client to be told a job has gone over quote because a senior had to spend more time on it than a junior.

Computerized time sheets with associated charge rates make it a very simple matter to print out a list of charge rates on any job at any particular time, providing the times are up to date. In the final analysis, there will be additions and deductions—known as write-offs—due to poor work, incorrect times, or failure to input times, which can create major problems of reconciliation.

Thus the need for:

- Weekly meetings with key staff in conjunction with an Action Sheet[1]
- Weekly tracking comparing actual times with the target on each job
- Weekly tracking comparing actual billings with target billings[2]
- A TARI benchmark that averages the various charge rates and simplifies the process of targeting and tracking, sustaining a clear view of the business from down in the trees that deals with the infinite complexities attending day-to-day events.

Done consistently, these things make it hard to miss target revenue and profit.

---

[1] For more information on the role of Action Sheets, see Chapter 22.
[2] Table 1-2 illustrates a simple format for tracking weekly results for comparison with target.

CHAPTER 15

Accounting Firm Wins by Losing a Third of Its Fees

Losing a client to a departing staff member is an ever-present concern for professional firms—a problem this practitioner succeeded in overcoming.

When the two partners of Jones & Associates reflected on the profession's advertising slogan, "Not Your Average Accountant," they considered their practice to be well above the average.

They practiced out of an upmarket office and ensured the latest magazines were available in a foyer staffed by a chic receptionist. They also offered regular seminars on matters related to client concerns, including taxation, retirement,

Chapter 15 | Accounting Firm Wins by Losing a Third of Its Fees

financial planning, computerization, management advice, and general consulting. Actively involved with community organizations, clubs, and church groups, they prided themselves on their marketing outreach.

Two matters, however, caused them nagging concern: the poor state of the bottom line when the time came to split profits two ways, and the potential loss of clients to departing staff members.

The individual share was only half of what partners of the other main practice in town took home. They knew this because of information passed on by the software consultant servicing both practices.

They reviewed their hourly charge rates, which were worked out in the traditional manner by multiplying salaries by 2.5; but as the fees were already higher than the other practice, the feeling was that they could not be increased.

This in turn made it difficult to reward existing staff members by paying them above-average salaries, a problem exacerbated by the recent departure of a long-serving staff member along with three valued clients.

They asked me if I could help.

"What are your total expenses?" I asked them as they handed me a large file of financial statements.

"Total expenses for the past year amounted to $2,200,000," said the junior partner.

"And what net profit did you end up with?"

"Close to $200,000, or about $100,000 each before tax," he added.

"And what surplus or net profit would you like to see to split between the two of you?"

"Well, we would like to see $300,000 each before tax, or $600,000 in total. Currently we're not getting anywhere near that."

I went to the whiteboard (Table 15-1).

Table 15-1. Targeting Gross Revenue for the Year Ending 20xx

A	Last Year's Expenses	$2,200,000
B	Last Year's Net Profit	$200,000
C = (A + B)	Last Year's Gross Revenue	$2,400,000
D	Potential Increase in Expenses	$200,000
E = (A + D)	Targeted Expenses	$2,400,000
F	Target Net Profit	$600,000
G = (E + F)	Target Gross Revenue	$3,000,000

Improving Profit

"So we are looking for a gross revenue of $3 million?" I asked, adding an expected rise in the cost of living index to the expenses and increasing the net profit to achieve the desired surplus of $600,000. "How many hours do you expect to bill to achieve that in the year?"

"We hope to get at least 64% of paid hours."

Paid hours for all the firm's employees totalled 31,250. Multiplied by 64%, the target billable hours worked out to 20,000, which divided into $3 million to give an average of $150 an hour (Table 15-2).

Table 15-2. Targeting Billable Hours and Average Fees for Year Ending 20xx

A	Paid Hours	31,250
B	Target Productivity	64%
C = (A × 64%)	Target Billable Hours	20,000
D	Target Gross Revenue	$3,000,000
E = (D ÷ C)	Target Average Fee	$150
F	Number of Working Weeks	45
G = (C ÷ F)	Target Average Hours Billed per Week	445[1]
H = (G × E)	Target Average Revenue per Week	$66,750

"It seems you are looking for an average of $150 an hour. Based on a 45-week year, it points to weekly average gross fees of 445 billed hours that, multiplied by $150, comes to nearly $67,000."

I explained the target average fee of $150 is best referred to a "target average rate index," or TARI for short, to emphasize it is a benchmark and not a fee or a cost.

"Even if we hold expenses down to last year's amount, I don't see that we can get anywhere near the targeted gross fees," the senior partner said with a sceptical note in his voice. "I think our real problem is having to write off a proportion of the invoiced amounts. I wouldn't be surprised if the total amounts to at least 10 percent or even 15 percent of the gross revenue."

"Yes," added the junior partner, "some of the work should really be done in less time and we really can't bill the clients for our slow work rate."

"Well," I said, "let's see what last year's productivity looks like if we apply the TARI of $150 to total billings."

---

[1] Rounded up from 444.4 hours.

Chapter 15 | Accounting Firm Wins by Losing a Third of Its Fees

I went to the whiteboard and wrote down the following (Table 15-3):

Table 15-3. Identifying Last Year's Productivity

A	Gross Revenue for Last Year	$2,400,000
B	New Target Average Rate Index (TARI)	$150/hour
C = (A ÷ B)	Hours Billed	16,000
D	Hours Paid	31,250
E = (C ÷ D × 100)	Productivity Percentage	51.2%
F = (E × 8 hours)	Billed Output per 8-Hour Day	4 hours, 6 minutes

"I see what you mean about having to write off a proportion of the invoiced bills," I said.

"Exactly," the senior partner exclaimed. "It seems to me we need to get on top of that matter before anything else."

"That will be no problem," I responded. "When you are about to bill a client, you divide the amount of the bill by the total number of hours spent by the various staff members as indicated in the software, and work out the average rate achieved."

I continued: "If it is under $150, you may want to review the time taken. If it is over $150, so much the better. Ideally, you will set a target of hours to complete the job before handing the job to a staff member."

One of the partners wondered whether they then needed to track hours on a daily basis.

"Yes," I said. "By midday each Thursday, you tally up the hours and rates to be invoiced out by 5 p.m. Friday in order to meet the hours targeted for the week. You write it up on the whiteboard in the staff room. If you look like you're under target, the staff will know what to do, particularly if they are placed on a bonus for every hour billed over target."

I discussed various ways of providing incentives to staff to sustain their interest and loyalty to the firm, and suggested they might think about giving certain staffers one-third of fees generated over and above 30 full hours of weekly billing.

The junior partner objected. "But that means letting the staff know the details of practice billings."

I smiled. "What they don't know they make up. Fear of their full participation will hold back the potential of the practice. The aim should be to harness their undivided input and energy. That is achieved by teamwork, with the whole practice focusing on target and cooperating to that end."

"But we only bill at the end of each month, and our software system only gives monthly reports." The junior partner sounded worried.

"Why wait until the end of a month if the job is ready for billing today? Try to bill weekly. Apart from improving your cash flow, you will maintain a firmer grip on hours and rate if they are monitored week by week."[2]

He continued to voice objections. "What about work in progress? Our hours may be spot on or over the target hours for the week, but they can't be billed because jobs are not completed."

"We are talking about billings only. If you use work-in-progress hours, you will have discrepancies when it comes to finalizing the account, bearing in mind you write off some of those hours if you feel the client may react adversely. Besides," I continued, "work in progress hours will tend to even themselves out when the time comes for billing. You will find write-offs will gradually fade away altogether as your team becomes focused on targeting how long a job should take before it is started."

I pointed out that nothing would happen unless they introduced an Action Sheet to monitor progress with the key staff on a weekly basis.[3]

The phone rang on the senior partner's desk. It was from the bright receptionist to say the taxi had arrived to take me to the airport.

Case Comment

As often happens, ambitious staff wanting a greater slice of the action leave for greener fields, and despite all contractual agreements they inevitably take some clients with them.

Conscious of this, the partners—once the write-off problems were under control—gave the staff the opportunity to earn a third of their billings and work largely at their own pace, with the proviso that they bill a minimum of 30 hours a week, net of any write-offs.

In the next six months, the practice increased its billings by 20% over the same period in the previous year and went on to outdo the targeted net profit per partner.

The 9-to-5 syndrome faded as staff began to enjoy the incentive of getting one-third of their individual charge-out rate for every hour billed over their personal 30-hour target, in a system where hours over the target were credited and hours under were debited, based on a three-month cycle.

---

[2] Table 1-2 illustrates a simple format for tracking weekly results for comparison with target.
[3] For information on the vital role of Action Sheets, see Chapter 22.

Within a year, the firm became the most profitable of all practices in the two-partner category.[4] It was a pleasure to visit and share in the positive and energizing atmosphere.

Software companies have long targeted the public accounting profession as a prime market for practice software and for the potential influence a practice has on its business clients. As a result, systems for timekeeping and charge-out rates have been fine-tuned to a high degree of sophistication. Time is usually costed and based on a minimum of 6-minute units, or 10 units an hour.

While the collation of times and the associated charge rate per client is a simple matter of inputting the client code, the actual billing is frequently subjected to the "feel" test. Is the bill too high and should it be written down? Or too low and should be written up? What was it last year? Has the client enjoyed an especially good year?

A practice targeting hours before processing the work will be in a position to compare target hours with time-sheet hours as per the computer printout.

If the practice has adopted TARI, it will be in a position to compare both time and rate for individual billings.

As most practices rely on monthly feedback from their software, there is seldom any weekly and accumulative comparison of time and rate charged with TARI. Reviews, if any, are held two to three weeks into the subsequent month, by which time it becomes all too difficult to recover from a poor result.

The legal practice in the following case study provides a change of pace.

---

[4]Interfirm comparison of accounting practices is made available within the profession.

CHAPTER 16

Legal Firm Transfers Productivity to the Bottom Line

Uncovering a major roadblock to productivity spurred this legal practitioner into clearing the backlog of files from the office floor.

When I first met Bill, he had been running his legal practice for 15 years or so. He said the pressures were unceasing and wondered how he could continue. Every year, he told his wife and children the need to work nights and weekends at home would cease and that things would get better.

As time passed, he employed additional staff to ease the burden and eventually a partner. If anything, the pressure increased.

I urged him to make the effort to attend a forthcoming Legal Practice Conference I had organized, and he promised to try. To my surprise he did

Chapter 16 | Legal Firm Transfers Productivity to the Bottom Line

attend, and I called on him some weeks later. The first thing I noticed was the absence of stacks of files that had previously cluttered the desk and floor of his office.

"What happened?" I asked.

"Well, the main thing that hit me," said Bill, "was that legal practices with the same staff and partner numbers as mine were bringing in double the fees, some treble. Mine was easily the lowest in fees per staff member. I think they called it 'inter-firm comparison.' I could not understand it, since we are so flat-out all the time and charge scale fees for most work, and I didn't seem to be doing anything noticeably different from the rest of them."

I nodded and he continued. "One of the speakers mentioned a study carried out by IBM, which showed the average typist only typed 8 words a minute during a typical day, due to many interruptions and so forth. It gave me an idea, so when I got back to the office I collected the printouts of all the work produced in my absence and counted the words input by the five clerical staff. Would you believe it worked out at 4 words a minute?

"Have a look at this." He drew out a sheet of paper from the drawer showing his analysis along the following lines (Table 16-1).

Table 16-1. Word Output per Minute

A	Number of Clerical Staff	5
B	Time available per Typist for 5 Days	30 hours
C = (A × B)	Total Time Available for 5 Staff	150 hours
D = (C × 60)	Number of Minutes	9,000 minutes
E	Total Output	36,000 words
F = (E ÷ D)	Output per Minute	4 words

I wondered if he appreciated that he had applied a classic piece of management science to his practice by undertaking such an objective measurement of activity.

He went on with growing excitement. "I called in Joan, the senior clerk, and put it to her that her team was inputting data at the rate of 4 words a minute. She would not have it at all. She said she and the others did at least 65 words a minute. I showed the evidence and pointed out how phone calls, cups of coffee for clients, and trips down the street for this and that eroded the time available for typing.

"I went out and purchased two Dictaphones,[1] one each for my partner and me and five transcribers, one for each clerk. I dictated my letters from then on and handed them to Joan, who organized the staff."

"How did that work out?" I asked.

"Well, it saved at least half the staff time previously taken up having to take notes. But they certainly didn't like the idea of being glued into earphones all day; they took days off for dubious sickies, banged doors loudly, stopped making tea and coffee, and generally made life pretty unbearable. In fact, it got so bad that my partner rang me late one evening and asked me to put everything back the way it had been because he couldn't stand it any longer. I agreed, and would have done so, but for an emergency court case that came up and I forgot all about the office for a few days. By the time I got back into harness, it had all seemed to come together, with the staff settled in to the new regime."

He leaned over the desk as though to emphasize the point: "Would you believe that I'm getting my letters back for signing on the same day that I dictated them?"

Waving an arm around to indicate a desk and floor now clear of files, he said, "I used to keep all the current files around me so as not to lose track."

"You mean you were unable to retrieve files easily?" I asked.

"No, it wasn't retrieval so much as keeping in touch with matters dictated that would come back to me for signing anything up to two weeks later. If I kept the file in the office, I would know it was waiting for a letter or a note."

"What do you intend to do now to make sure things don't slip back?" I queried.

"I'm going to look at improving the accounts to see if we can do interim billing instead of waiting until matters have reached a conclusion, many months later." He spoke as a man with renewed energy, new life, and a motivation to grasp it. His enthusiasm was infectious.

"You know, Bill, you didn't have to wait for 15 years and an almost failed family life and business to go with it." I said.

"Well if someone had told me about 8 words a minute 15 years ago, I guess I wouldn't have gone through all the pain."

---

[1] Yes, this case happened well over a decade ago. However, I have it on good authority that there are still a lot of Dictaphones in use by old-school attorneys who have not caught up with the times.

"I'm not referring to the 8 words a minute, helpful though that has been. I'm referring to setting up a clear target of what you need to achieve to cover expenses, including a reasonable take-home salary plus some profit."

"I can only do my best."

"Well, let's look ahead and see if we can pinpoint what that 'best' represents in terms of profit to two partners."

"Happily," he agreed.

"First step is run through the expenses." Referring to previous statements, we wrote down every item according to Bill's estimates for the year ahead. The total came to $850,000.

"What would you like to make to cover partner salaries and profit for blood, sweat, tears, and risk?" I asked.

"A bit more than last year?" he said tentatively.

"A lot more if you consider the increased productivity you have released. If you only achieve an extra 10 hours a day from your five staff, think what that means over 12 months!"

Looking at the resources available to achieve these fees, I suggested the two partners target 1,500 billable hours each, and that five staffers could target average billable hours of 1,400 hours each, making a total of 10,000 hours (Table 16-2).

Table 16-2. Targeting Performance for the Year Ending 20XX

A	Total Expenses	$850,000
B	Target Net Profit	$350,000
C = (A + B)	Target Gross Revenue	$1,200,000
D = (2 × 1,500 hours)	Target Billable Hours, 2 Partners	3,000
E = (C ÷ D)	Target Average Fee per Partner	$400[2]
F = (5 × 1,400 hours)	Target Billable Hours, 5 Staff	7,000
G = (D + F)	Target Total Hours, Partners and Staff	10,000
H = (C ÷ G)	Target Average Fee per Hour	$120

---

[2] In some legal practices, the partner's charge rate is inclusive of input from support staff—thus the $400 per hour should Bill and his partner wish to operate along those lines. However, their preference was to include the support staff in order to encourage a greater sense of participation in a team effort.

"The target average fee of $120 is the TARI or target average rate index we discussed at the conference, do you remember?"

"Yes, of course—you rubbed it in enough! It's a benchmark for comparing our fees. The average hourly rate of $120 across the board seems to be about what we are getting on scale fees," he said.

I elaborated: "The difference now will be the level of productivity. Right now we need to establish a simple feedback system to capture your billings on a week-by-week basis."

"I understand," said Bill, "but we usually send out our bills at the end of each month, and some matters can't really be billed until they are finished. In any case, we don't always use hours to work the fees out. We sometimes apply the fee scales indicated by the Law Society."

"It would help your liquidity to bill where possible at the end of each week rather than wait for the end of the month," I replied. "As for tracking the hours when using scale fees, this can be done by dividing the billing by $120 to calculate what accountants call standard hours."

"But what about work in progress—surely that represents hours of input?"

"Yes it does, but you can't pay bills with work in progress."

I showed him a weekly performance summary sheet that would enable him to track results against target each week and accumulatively.

"Is this a sort of interfirm thing?" he asked.

"No, Bill. This has to do with achieving the potential of this business, given its expense structure and partner take-home expectations. It could well be that the resulting average gross fee per staff member is comparable with the average for the profession, but bear in mind the interfirm data is a statistic of a collection of firms operating in a variety of locations and with a varying mix of work."

Bill's eyes lit up as he began to understand that, just as he increased the typist's productivity, by tracking hours he could legitimately increase the number of hours billed.

I continued: "The target billings of $1,200,000, represent a first cut, as it were. As the weekly information feeds back, the picture will become clearer, and enable a second or third cut to be made. Meanwhile, you need to track weekly and accumulatively along the following lines" (Table 16-3).

Table 16-3. Tracking Results Week Ending _____

Date	Invoice Number A	Fees ($) B	Number of Units (Hours) C	Average per Unit ($) D = (B ÷ C)
6/4	3876	3,500	32	110
6/11	3877	9,000	70	129
6/18	3878	2,500	22	114
6/25	3879	5,000	51	98
Total		**20,000**	**175**	**114**
Total to date		360,000	3,025	119
Target to date		**380,000**	**3,167**	**120**
Variance +/-		−20,000	−142	−1

Note If the hours have not been tracked, then the fees are divided by TARI to provide calculated or "standard" hours.

I wrote out an Action Sheet, and pinpointed who was to do what and by when.

Case Comment

Charge-out rates, calculated and applied in similar fashion to accountants and architects, would quickly drive managing partners into the trees, where they tend to get lost in the detail. Thus, the need for a sustained view of the woods, such as TARI provides.

Even if time sheets are not kept, fees divided by TARI will provide an overview of "standard" hours, which, if accumulated by the week, will very quickly pinpoint the level of chargeable hours compared with available hours. For example, assume fees charged out this week amounted to $2,400. Dividing this by a TARI of $120 would indicate 10 "standard" hours billed.

Assume after 4 weeks the accumulation of weekly fees amounted to $9,600; dividing by $120 would indicate a billing of 80 "standard" hours in total, compared with a target of, say, 120 billable hours (4 weeks × 30 hours a week).

Once a main source of fees in many legal practices, conveyancing (doing the legal paperwork relating to property sales) has been subjected to fierce competition, putting practices under financial pressure. So the need for targeting and tracking revenue has become a growing imperative for profitable survival.

Noting the likely time a matter will absorb and multiplying by TARI will provide an estimate of the likely fee. Comparison of the estimate with the final fee will focus attention on where the rubber meets the road.

As the following real-life case illustrates, the effectiveness of such an approach is not limited to professions such as architecture, accounting, and law.

CHAPTER 17

Contractor Increases Strike Rate to 1 in 4

A large air conditioning group teaches its contractors how to quote to win installations. One contractor quoted differently

A manufacturer of commercial and home air conditioning units was conducting two-day seminars in five states. A total of 120 installation contractors attended.

The purpose of the seminars was to improve management skills related to finance, systems, marketing, staff motivation, and training. The manufacturer believed that improving these skills would strengthen the contractors and ultimately help them sell more of their AC units.

The manufacturer had called me in to participate. To drive home the difference between the traditional approach to quoting a job and quoting a job based on the concepts underlying Contribution-Based Activity, I asked the participants to individually work out and hand in a quote for the installation of a commercial unit costing the contractor $3,000 and requiring an estimated six production-hours to install.

Chapter 17 | Contractor Increases Strike Rate to 1 in 4

Using the method advocated by the manufacturer, participants marked-up the cost of the unit by 33%, and added a cost to cover labor along the lines shown in Table 17-1:

Table 17-1. Job Quote: Manufacturer's Method

A	Cost of Air Conditioning Unit	$3,000
B = (A + 33%)	Cost + $1,000 Markup	$4,000
C	Time to Install	6 hours
D	Hourly Charge Rate	$50
E = (C x D)	Installation cost	$300
F = (B + E)	Quote for Installation	$4,300

Quotes ranged between $4,100 and $4,600. Asked how they worked out their hourly charge rates, they said they applied a percentage to the hourly wage to cover overhead. It was noticeable that across all participants, neither the wage rate nor the added percentage varied significantly.

It happened to be on the final day of the five seminars when, among the quotes handed in, was one for $3,480.

It was so different that I asked the contractor concerned to identify himself in order to explain how he arrived at such a low rate compared with his colleagues.

A tall, suntanned contractor in his mid-thirties stood up. "I owe it to my accountant," he said. "I used to mark up like all the others and I was winning about 1 in every 15 quotes. One day, he suggested I compare quotes with a targeted average hourly rate as a benchmark, the same as he did. He called it the TARI approach or something like that. In this case, where no special problems were involved, I merely used the average rate."

"The accountant was referring to the target average rate index, or TARI for short," I explained, delighted to hear of an accountant "out there" who had grasped the concept and applied it to his clients' quotes.

"Would you like to tell us how you worked out your benchmark rate?" I asked him, offering him the marking pen and indicating the whiteboard.

He walked to the front of the class confidently. "We worked out what my expenses were likely to be for the year," he said as he took the pen, "and added a good profit to it. We divided the total by the hours I thought we would be charging out for the same period."

Table 17-2 shows what he put up on the board.

Table 17-2. Developing a TARI Benchmark

A	Total Expenses	$125,000
B	Target Profit	$75,000
C = (A + B)	Target Contribution	$200,000
D	Target Billable Hours	2,500 hours
E = (C ÷ D)	Target Average Rate Index (TARI)	$80

He said, "That's why my quote came in at $480 plus the cost of the unit. Six hours by $80 were based on two to inspect and quote, four to install."

"Has it made a difference to your strike rate in quoting?"

"Yes, I now win one in four, and I'm well ahead of target for the year." he smiled broadly as he sat down.

"Hang on," said a voice loudly from the back of the room. "So you don't add *any* mark up to the unit? Why not?"

The gentleman stood up again. "Because when I did, I might win on some jobs with expensive equipment and lose on others with cheaper equipment. It was pot luck, really. Apart from that, I was quoting against other contractors who marked up their equipment in the same way. That was why I was only winning 1 in 15 quotes compared to 1 in 4 now; it's because I know what I need for an hour on the job."

I then asked him how he kept track of hours charged out. "The accountant gets me to put the hours on the copies of each invoice with the cost of the material, and I drop them over to him once a week. He works out how I am going against target and keeps me apprised.

"You don't keep the records yourself, then?"

"I started to, but I fell behind until I lost track. He keeps me up to it."

I referred the group to an example of the tracking matrix in the seminar notes (Table 17-3).

Chapter 17 | Contractor Increases Strike Rate to 1 in 4

Table 17-3. Tracking Results Week Ending _____

Day	Sales ($) A	Cost of Materials ($) B	Gross Profit contribution ($) C = (A − B)	Contribution (%) D = (C ÷ A)	No. of Hours E	Average Gross Profit per hour F = (C ÷ E)
1	9,400	7,800	1,600	17	16	100
5	10,000	8,500	1,500	15	20	75
Total	19,400	16,300	3,100	16	36	86
Previous Total	171,400	143,976	27,424	16	269	102
New Total	190,800	160,276	30,524	16	304	100
Target	176,000	150,400	25,600	15	320	80
Variance	+14,800	+10.276	+4,924	+1	−16	+20

Case Comment

I was asked to address a meeting of the plumbing industry, some of whom were also engaged in installing air conditioning as well as all manner of pipe laying. There were about 270 in attendance. Handing out blank sheets of paper, I asked them to write out a quote for a job for which the materials and parts cost $2,000 with an estimated labor time of 10 hours. The quotes were collected and summarized during the coffee break.

When they had settled back in their seats, I asked those with an hourly rate exceeding $80 an hour to indicate by raising their hands. No hand was raised and there was general laughter as though I must be dreaming to think they had an hourly rate that high.

I then asked for those with an hourly rate exceeding $60 an hour to raise their hands. More laughter and no hands raised.

At rates exceeding $50 an hour, a few did raise their hands.

At rates exceeding $40 an hour, hands went up everywhere.

"Well, you would be interested to know the average hourly rate for the 130 quotes handed in was $100," I told them.

There was stunned silence. "All of the quotes without exception marked up the materials with an average of 33%, making $660 contribution. If we divide that by the 10 hours we get an additional contribution of $66 an hour. When this is added to what you call your hourly charge-out rate, which averages $35 to $40, you can see how the result works out to $100-plus." I wrote it on the whiteboard (Table 17-4).

Table 17-4. Determining the Effective Hourly Charge Rate

A	Average Quote	$3,000
B	Cost of Materials	$2,000
C = (A − B)	Contribution[1]	$1,000
D	Time for Job	10 hours
E = (C ÷ D)	Average Rate per Hour	$100

I couldn't help wondering why we have allowed ourselves to be so deluded by the traditional accounting approach; we can no longer see the woods for the trees.

As with any business, the objective is to cover expenses and make a profit. The traditional approach to achieving that objective is to add a percentage markup to materials plus a planned number of billable hours.

Jobs with less material content taking 10 hours result in less contribution than jobs with high material content taking the same time.

To the extent that planning an hourly charge rate for the year ahead calls for a guesstimate of the cost of materials used in the previous year, there is further uncertainty. This is particularly the case if tracking results against plan, or is not carried out weekly and accumulatively.

A business operating without a markup on materials, and focused on targeting and tracking enough billable hours weekly and accumulatively to achieve the desired contribution, is far more likely to succeed.

In the final analysis, as this and other case studies reveal, providing a clear focus on the two levers of contribution and unit activity is far more likely to result in achieving and sustaining a competitive edge.

As I prepared to leave the venue that day, a plumber stopped me. "Can you spare a minute?" he asked. "They talked about the need to market your business today and I can't see how that's possible with the work my firm does."

"What sort of work do you do?" I queried.

"Plumbing, but mainly underground, you know, sewage piping."

"What buildings have you worked on around here?"

---

[1]Contribution toward covering expenses plus profit of the business. Often referred to as *gross profit contribution*.

Chapter 17 | Contractor Increases Strike Rate to 1 in 4

He thought for a moment. "Well, there's the IBM building," he said, referring to a state-of-the-art local skyscraper.

"Great," I replied. "Put a photo of it on a flyer to advertise your firm."

"But we only worked on the piping system below ground!"

"All the more reason for the photo," I said. "Who would want to work in a building with no toilets?"

CHAPTER 18

Hot Bread Baker Discovers More to Bread than Flour

Until he came face-to-face with the added value in bread and sausage rolls, the proprietor was actively seeking additional products to boost the bottom line

Ushered in by the accountant, the baker came into the conference room accompanied by his wife, looking a little tired and weary. It was late afternoon, and he had been up since before dawn in his bakery. A residue of flour whitened his eyebrows and clung to the back of his arms.

The previous evening, I had addressed a client gathering of an accounting practice and he was one of several requesting an interview.

He kicked off the conversation. "I came to see what you reckoned about my idea of leasing a pie-making machine. I can get one that makes 4,000 pies an hour, and they reckon I can flog them to a wholesaler for 70 cents each. Make a fortune. What do you reckon?"

"Who is 'they'?" I asked, knowing 70 cents was above the price paid by retailers, let alone wholesalers.

"The machine people," he fired back. "They should know, being in the business an' all that."

"Well, before going into that, do you think we could spend a moment looking at what you do right now?" I said, steering him away from what I decided would be a prolonged and futile debate. "How many do you employ?"

"Me and an apprentice pastry cook in the back, and the wife and a part-time assistant in the shop."

"How many loaves of bread do you make in an hour?" I queried.

"A hundred-ten," he said without hesitation.

"And what do you sell a loaf for?"

"A dollar-sixty."

"And how much do the ingredients cost?"

"Twenty-four cents."

I wrote the figures on the whiteboard (Table 18-1).

Table 18-1. Unit[1] Contribution from Bread

A	Retail Sale Price Loaf of Bread	$1.60
B	Cost of Ingredients	$0.24
C = (A − B)	Contribution per Loaf	$1.36
D	Number of Loaves per Hour	110
E = (D × C)	Total Contribution	$150[2]
F = (E ÷ 2)	Unit Contribution [3]	$75[4]

"That works out at $150 gross profit an hour or $75 per man-hour if we take account of the apprentice," I observed. "What about bread rolls—how many of those do you make in an hour?"

"Six hundred sixty-six," he said without a second's thought, "and they sell for 30 cents and the ingredients cost 4 cents."

---

[1] A unit of activity is a man-hour in this business.
[2] Rounded from $149.60.
[3] The baker plus the apprentice pastry cook equates to an hour each.
[4] Rounded from $74.80.

I multiplied 26 cents by 666.

"That works out at $173 gross per hour, or $86.50 per man-hour," I said. "What about sausage rolls?"

His response came like shots from a gun: "Six hundred an hour selling for 90 cents and ingredients 10 cents."

"That works out at $480 gross an hour or $240 per man-hour," I said, multiplying 600 by 80 cents and dividing by 2. The accountant, who had been observing quietly to this point, permitted a faint smile to crease his features.

"Ah, but the lamingtons are my best bet!" the baker exclaimed. Lamingtons are a traditional Australian dessert. "I've got a wholesaler who'll take all the lamingtons I can make." His eyes lit up at the thought.

"How many do you make?" I asked

He had to stop and discuss that with his wife, who had been sitting placidly beside him.

"Two hundred-fifty an hour," he said, "selling for 65 cents retail and 25 cents wholesale. Ingredients, 8 cents."

"How many do you sell retail compared with wholesale?" I asked.

"Probably three-quarters wholesale and a quarter retail."

I quickly calculated the outcome as I went to the whiteboard (Table 18-2).

Table 18-2. Analysis of Wholesale and Retail Sales of Lamingtons

Wholesale:		
A	Wholesale Price	25 cents × (250 × 3/4) = $47
B	Ingredients	8 cents × (250 × 3/4) = $15
C = (A − B)	Contribution	17 cents × (250 × 3/4) = $32
Retail:		
A	Retail Price	65 cents × (250 × 1/4) = $41
B	Ingredients	8 cents × (250 × 1/4) = $5
C = (A − B)	Contribution	57 cents × (250 × 1/4) = $36

"Given it takes you and the apprentice to produce a batch, if you sold the full 250 output wholesale it works out to approximately $42 or $21 contribution per man-hour." I did the math on the whiteboard:

250 × 17 cents = $42.50 ÷ 2 = $21.25 per man hour

"If you sold the lot retail it works out to $142.50 or $71.75 per man-hour." I did the math once again:

250 × 57 cents = $142.50 ÷ 2 = $71.25 per man hour.

He looked dumbfounded until he remembered something: "Ah, but I've got plans for a machine that will make them a lot faster!"

I ignored that for the time being. It was time to plan ahead. Given the fragmentary data available, there was little point carrying the analysis any further.

We reviewed the expenses of the total bakery and, excluding ingredients, arrived at a guesstimated $125,000. His profit the previous year amounted to $25,000. However, given the obvious potential, he was inspired to project a bottom line of $100,000, making a target gross profit of $225,000.

Given a total availability of 4,500 hours in the bakery, and his belief that 75% of those hours would be productive, we targeted 72% or 3,250 hours for the planned period, amounting to a TARI of $69.23 or close to $70 per man-hour (Table 18-3).

Table 18-3. Targeting Next Year's Performance

A	Target Expenses	$125,000
B	Target Profit	$100,000
C = (A + B)	Target Contribution	$225,000
D	Productive Hours (4,500 × 72%)	3,250
E = (C ÷ D)	Target Average Contribution per Hour	$69.23

I pointed out that the target average contribution, better known as the target average rate index or TARI, is in effect a benchmark against which the unit-contribution of other products can be compared. "I can see that," he said peering at the figures, "but I think we're going to need the pie-making machine to get a $100,000 profit!"

"Did the pie machine company guarantee to buy the output for 70 cents a pie?" I asked.

"Well, more or less," he said.

"Not really, dear," his wife noted in a gentle tone.

"Well, they said there would be no problem," he added sternly.

I suggested that a pie machine capable of turning out 4,000 pies an hour would probably cost between $250,000 to $500,000, depending whether it included the preparation of the pastry, associated fillings, pie molding, and heating facilities. The leasing cost alone would be in the region of $50,000 to $100,000 a year; and if—as was likely—the pie machine company failed to buy the output, it would be necessary to take on at least one and more likely two sales representatives to sell the pies.

"Before making any decision about the pie machine or, indeed, the lamington machine," I concluded, "what say we track results daily for a while, and see how the business performs against target?"

The baker's wife nodded, and he sighed in reluctant agreement.

Picking up the Action Sheet (Table 18-4), we decided who should do what by when.

Table 18-4. Action Sheet

Date	Item	Action	Who	When
3/1	Daily Sales	Record daily by product, cost of ingredients, and hours	BB	3/10
3/2	Daily Sales	Prepare format for recording daily sales	AC	3/10
3/3	Next Meeting		BB, AC	4/9

Present at meeting: BB, AC, KC

The baker agreed to keep a daily record of the product baked and numbers sold, and to e-mail the results each week to the accountant, who would enter the data and e-mail back a comparison with target.

We then scheduled a meeting with the accountant in four weeks to review progress and make any necessary adjustments to the plan, including the TARI of about $70 per hour.

Knowing the baker would have difficulty in designing an appropriate format to record production and sales, the accountant agreed to prepare the sheet and deliver it the following day.

Case Comment

It is doubtful if more than one baker in a thousand has a clear picture of contribution per hour[5] of baking input. As a result, it becomes largely a matter of bakers' instinct as to additional products taken on or rejected.

While this baker agreed to target an output absorbing 75% of available hours, he really had no idea of his current level of productivity.

---

[5] Contribution per hour or unit-contribution, where the unit refers to one production-hour—in this industry, a man-hour.

In this case, he was selling output at retail price in the shop front. That made all the difference. Had he been selling at wholesale prices, the contribution would have been much less.

It was a simple matter to draft a matrix comparing actual output with each hour of input. (Table 18-5).[6]

Table 18-5. Summary of Products Sales: Day _____ Week Ending _____

Product	Sale Price	Ingredients	Contribution	Units (Hours)	Average per Unit
Bread 1					
Bread 2					
Bread 7					
Rolls 1					
Rolls 2					
Cakes 1					
Cakes 2					
Cakes 6					
Other					
Day Total					
Total b/f					
Week's Total					
Total to Date b/f					
New Total c/f					
Target					$70
Variance +/-					

The key to making it happen would be implementation: everything would be dependent upon the level of persistence the accountant exercised in extracting the weekly record.

Fortunately, the accountant seemed quite confident. "I don't expect too much trouble collecting the data," he grinned, nodding toward an attractive junior staff member with a bright, smiling personality. "I've got my best new recruit on the job."

---

[6]This matrix is of course adaptable to many businesses.

The accountant told me later in the year that the process of relating daily output to contribution per man-hour had boosted the bottom line and refocused the client's ambition for expansion to one of experimenting with ways and means of improving the contribution.

In all, a positive outcome for the business, for the accountant and not least, the baker's wife who, over the years, had become immune to her husband's bright ideas and carried on as best she was able in the front of shop.

The next chapter demonstrates how a bright idea by a CEO of a major corporate can also go astray.

CHAPTER 19

Window Manufacturer's Flawed Foundation

The fabricator who put the window frames together was the most productive of anyone on the assembly floor. It wasn't his fault the method of assembly was inefficient

Having successfully acquired a patented aluminum extrusion for making aluminum window frames with greater structural strength, a nationwide company established a new plant complete with factory, production, engineering, fabricating, marketing, and distribution staff, and commenced an extensive advertising campaign.

Chapter 19 | Window Manufacturer's Flawed Foundation

Consultants were commissioned to set up appropriate systems and procedures, from the acquisition of raw materials to the installation of finished products in buildings.

Twelve months down the track, orders were few and far between and the marketing team was under scrutiny by the CEO. He knew the product was new, but it had been tried and tested and was well accepted in Europe.

He accepted that the lead time in getting any new product on the market varied, but with the heavy advertising expenditure over the past year, coupled with all the promotions that had taken place, it was time to expect a greater flow of orders than they were getting.

He did not agree that the price tag was too high. That had been well and truly looked at by the finance team.

I was introduced to this debate as a trainee consultant attached to the senior consultant on the job. He gave me a stopwatch and, as an exercise, told me to "work study"[1] the window frame-making process going on in the plant. Apart from my need for training, it was a useful way of getting me out of the senior consultant's hair for a week or so.

I was introduced to an employee engaged in fabricating large aluminum frames for a major urban building project. The foreman explained to him that it was a matter of me getting on-the-job work experience and that there was nothing sinister in my noting the time it took for each step of the process.

After five days of work studying what seemed to be a laborious process of assembling one window frame a day, it was time to compile a report on my findings for the senior consultant. I collated all the data and averaged the times for each movement from the point of taking the extrusions from the rack to a completed frame.

Apart from gaining a fairly accurate assessment of the assembly process, I also gained an insight into the life and times of a friendly fabricator.

In the plant engineer's office, I set up a scaled-down representation of the fabrication on the basis of one quarter-inch on the board representing 36 inches in the plant.

I hammered in four 2-inch nails to represent the two trestles on which the window lengths were placed for riveting with inlays and end pieces.

I hammered another nail in to represent the washroom location, and another for the extrusion rack where the aluminum lengths and inlays were stacked each morning, ready for assembly.

---

[1] Work study involved looking at the method of construction as well as the timing of each activity involved.

Taking a ball of string, and referring to my work-study sheets, I began tracing the pathway of the fabricator, as he picked up a length of aluminum, placed it on the trestles, riveted it to a crosspiece, walked down to the other end and repeated the process. Occasionally he would drop tools for a visit to the washroom, now represented by that nail on the drawing.

The ball of string ran out and I tied the end onto a new ball. When the second ball of string ran out, I had to ask the foreman to send down the road for additional balls. Meanwhile, I replaced the 2-inch nails with 4-inch nails.

I continued the process until the string ran over the 4-inch nail heads and longer nails were needed to replace them. It took 12 balls of string woven backward and forward over 6-inch nails to complete the miniature replica of fabricating one window frame. The result looked like a nest of spiders had spun a huge pyramid on the drawing board. I calculated the distance walked to be five miles.[2]

The senior consultant was not amused. "You must have included assembly for five days instead of averaging the times!"

I assured him the times and method had been averaged to represent one window.

Word got around, and the factory manager came to look at this phenomenon displayed in the drawing office. When he saw it, he shrugged his shoulders and walked off without a word. Every day he parked his car in a corner of the plant and walked past the fabrication process, but apparently saw nothing untoward.

My friend the fabricator who worked on the window was astounded that he walked five miles a day. He wondered if that was the cause of his varicose vein problem and railed against the length of string that tracked his visits to and from the washroom.

During their three weekly visits to the plant, the finance and marketing directors made a point of checking out this piece of research they had heard about, and they wanted me to explain it to them.

The finance director studied it carefully and looked puzzled, while the marketing director began to get excited. "I'd like one of these made up for each of my reps," he said.

"Why so?" asked the finance director.

"Well, when people see what goes into making these windows, they'll understand why it takes so long and costs so much!"

---

[2] Or eight kilometers.

Challenged by the whole exercise, I spent time working out a preassembly method that cut the distance the fabricator walked down to half a mile, and the assembly time by two-thirds.

To me it was a revelation. Here was a nationwide corporation embarking on a major campaign at no small expense, and yet at the very foundation was a serious crack undermining its potential. Everybody saw it, but nobody really saw it. It was all too familiar.

In retrospect, it seemed extraordinary that no one had checked with their European counterparts to find out how they put their windows together, or even how long the fabrication of various configurations should take.

Had they done so, it would have been possible to establish a targeted gross profit contribution benchmark per hour[3] as a focus for quoting and pricing decisions.

Case Comment

Both the factory and production managers parked their cars in a corner of the factory and walked past the window fabrication every day. Anxious to get to their desks to tackle the daily workload, they saw it, but did not see it as it really was.

The senior consultant of the consulting firm, my training supervisor, was up to his eyeballs working with the production manager scheduling purchases and calculating logistics for a nationwide push of the product. He also did not see the problem.

The finance and IT departments were busy preparing a more updated accounts package to cope with the expected demand, and therefore the thought never occurred to them.

The marketing department, whose enthusiasm had been somewhat dented by production delays on large buildings, was "head down and tail up" working up a long-term promotional strategy for tackling the small-home market, which they hoped would develop sales in non-structural aluminum windows.

Had I known then about contribution-based activity, target average rate index (TARI) benchmarks, invoice sampling, and so forth, it would have been but a matter of minutes to identify and illustrate the weakness threatening survival of a potentially profitable business.[4]

---

[3] Best known as *target average rate index*, or *TARI*, to emphasize its benchmark status.
[4] Failure to seamlessly relate the fabricator's $20 hourly wage to the gross profit contribution per hour remains a blind spot at the heart of current commercial information systems to this day.

For example, assume the target contribution of the window frame department was $2,000,000 and the unit of activity driving fabrication was a production-hour contributing $100 an hour (Table 19-1).

Table 19-1. Developing a Target Average Rate Index Benchmark for Product X

A	Target Expenses (excluding materials)	$1,500,000
B	Target Profit	$500,000
C = (A + B)	Target Contribution	$2,000,000
D	Target Units of Billable Activity	20,000 production-hours
E = (C ÷ D)	Target Average Rate Index (TARI)	$100

Is it likely management would not have been so casual about a fabrication process taking three times longer than it needed to, had they been aware of the connection between a targeted $100 contribution and a $20 per hour wage.[5]

In such a case, because the process was taking at least three times longer than intended, the targeted contribution of $100 would have been reduced to $33[6]—a result that would have become apparent within a week or two.

As a result of the work study, the fabrication process was changed, output improved, expenses were contained, and profits began to flow.

It remains a matter for reflection as to whether the positive reaction by the decision makers would have been so immediate, had it not been for the extraordinary sight of 6-inch nails covered with the equivalent of five miles of string.

---

[5]In Chapter 4, the financial implications of failure to grasp the connection between wage and contribution for the same production-hour is driven home to the CEO.
[6]$100 ÷ 3 = $33.33.

CHAPTER 20

Multi-Home Contractor Discovers a New Way Home

From the design to the completed house, all looked good on paper, but slippage was occurring. Figuring a way to make the supervisors more accountable turned the situation around

The contractor was angry. "I sold and built 75 homes last year, all selected from one of our designs, all subcontracted out to the trades, and all, in theory, giving me a 10 percent margin. At an average of $13,300 for each home, I should have made a million to cover office overhead and profit."

"What did you make?" I asked from the other side of a very large teak desk.

"Nowhere near enough to keep the bank off my back! The account is a quarter of a million worse off than this time last year."

"Do you have much owing to you?"

"Receivables are about level with payables," he sighed.

"Are you paying more for your materials and subcontractors than you planned?"

"The estimator reckons we are on track, but I don't know whether he can keep up with it. I mean, he's got all his quantities and prices on tap, and orders the materials to site and so on, but the accounts do not always identify what went where, and everything is put into the one bucket."

He paused to contain his exasperation, then continued. "He complains that he doesn't get informed about what is happening on site, and in any case, we are always pressing him for a quote for a potential buyer. We might win one out of five quotes. It's pretty tough competition out there."

I asked, "How many additional houses could you have built if you had won more quotes?"

"Any number," he said. "It's a matter of employing another one or more supervisors."

"How many houses can a supervisor handle?" I asked.

"That depends on the design, local terrain, and location. Some are way out of town and take half a day traveling to get there and back. I'd say ours are pretty flat-out handling 15 a year each."

It was a scenario where phones rang ceaselessly. Subcontractors had to be kept busy or they would be unavailable when required, the right materials had to be on site on time, and work had to be coordinated to meet scheduled council inspections or be held up.

Predesigned plans needed to be adjusted to meet varying ground levels and soils in different locations, progress payments had to be attended to, and discontented customers placated. This often required adjustments to plan—despite the most comprehensively prepared contracts—leading to additional unpaid work. Things had gotten out of control.

"Let's look ahead," I said, "and quantify where we'd like to be in a year's time, and then decide how we are going to get there." I reached for a blank sheet of paper.

I continued: "We'll list the overheads you have mentioned and guesstimate any increases or decreases in the expenses needed to keep the office open and the business functioning at its current level."

The projected overhead expenses of $750,000 included salaries for five supervisors, the estimator, accountant, receptionist, two sales reps, and two clerical assistants.

When I asked the contractor for input about a desirable net profit, he shrugged his shoulders and dubiously agreed to my suggestion of $250,000, giving a planned gross profit of $1,000,000 (Table 20-1).

Table 20-1. Planning Year Ending _____

A	Total Expenses	$750,000
B	Net Profit	$250,000
C = (A + B)	Contribution[1]	$1,000,000

"Normally," I said, "when tracking actual results against planned results, we would identify the desired average contribution per unit of key activity. One view of the key activity here could be the number of houses. Assuming the same number as last year, that would mean a benchmark of $13,333 per house, for example (Table 20-2).

Table 20-2. Identifying the Benchmark

A	Target Contribution	$1,000,000
B	Target Number of Houses	75
C = (A ÷ B)	**Target Average Contribution**	**$13,333**

I explained that the average contribution of $13,333 would be referred to as a "target average rate index," or TARI, to emphasize its benchmark status.

"We just add 10 percent to the total cost," he said, "and it comes out pretty close to that number."

"Well, adding $13,333 is not too different from the way you have been operating—looking to get a margin on each house sufficient to cover expenses and profit. The idea of a margin on top of costs is fair enough, but its success is dependent on how effectively costs are controlled. Obviously, when costs end up close to, or more than, the contract price of the house, you are in trouble."

"Tell me about it!" the contractor said with a grin, finally loosening up a bit.

---

[1] *Contribution,* frequently referred to as *gross profit,* is the sum left over to cover expenses and profit after paying for materials.

Chapter 20 | Multi-Home Contractor Discovers a New Way Home

"A more effective approach is to identify the supervisor's time as the key activity. In this case, five supervisors would have an estimated chargeable time of, say, 6 hours a day for 5 days a week for 45 weeks.[2] This amounts to 1,350 hours per supervisor or 6,750 hours for five supervisors. We can work out a TARI benchmark accordingly" (Table 20-3).

Table 20-3. Planning and Targeting Performance Year Ending _____

A	Number of Supervisors	5
B	Billable Units[3] per Supervisor	1,350 hours
C = (A × B)	Total Billable Units	6,750 hours
D	Target Contribution	$1,000,000
E = (D ÷ C)	Target Average Rate Index (TARI)	$148
F	Number of Houses	75
G = (C ÷ F)	Target Billable Hours per House	90 hours
H = (E × G)	Target Contribution per House	$13,320

"Translating this back into plain language and given an estimated 75 houses, it means each supervisor has an average of 90 hours per home to make up the chargeable hours of 1,350 hours per supervisor," I explained.

"I wouldn't have thought we need 90 hours' supervision for every house," the contractor said, in contradiction to his earlier remarks about 15 houses a year per supervisor. "I'm surprised to hear it. After all, the sub-trades have been with us long enough to know what we expect. We plan six weeks per house and I would expect an average of eight hours' supervision a week would be maximum. It's not as though every house is a new design."

"Do you mean your supervisors are underemployed or could manage to supervise more houses?" I asked.

"Well they always seem to be flat-out so I can't say they are underemployed. I guess I haven't really had time to put my mind to the matter, what with the downturn of the economy, inflation, bank pressures, and so on."

I said, "If the supervision hours per house should be closer to 50 hours as you indicated, it suggests the supervisors are somewhat unproductive."

"How so?"

I pulled out a clean sheet of paper and began writing (Table 20-4).

---

[2] 52 weeks, less 4 weeks' annual leave, 2 weeks' (10 working days) public holidays, and 1 week's sick leave.
[3] The key unit of activity is one hour.

Table 20-4. Estimating Productivity

A	Number of Houses	75
B	Supervisory Hours per House	50
C = (A × B)	Total Supervisory Hours	3,750
D	Supervisors' Hours Available[4]	6,750
E = (C ÷ D × 100)	Productivity A	55.5%
F = (5 × 1,800 hours)	Supervisors' Paid Hours	9,000
G = (C ÷ F × 100)	Productivity B	41.7%[5]

Driving home the need to look more closely at productivity, I compared the 50 supervisory hours per house with both the available hours and the paid hours.

"Well, at least on paper, there would seem to be supervisory time available for more houses," I pointed out.

He looked puzzled. "What do you suggest?"

"I suggest we make the supervisors more accountable for their time," I said. "On the face of it, you don't need five of them, but before doing anything about that, let's give them a target of 50 hours a house, based on 8 hours a week for 6 weeks. We can track results and get a fix on the average contribution per hour achieved by each of them."

"I'm not sure how they will go along with it," he said.

"Well, let's try and see how it goes," I replied, making the point that a supervisor was standing in much the same place as an independent building contractor and, as such, would be well placed to earn a bonus per completed house once the contribution exceeded target.

The first step was to develop a target average rate index (TARI) based on 50 supervisory hours per house as the key units of activity (Table 20-5).

---

[4]Available hours take account of travel time and other administrative tasks not directly connected with the supervision of any particular house construction.
[5]41.7% of an 8-hour day = 3 hours and 20 minutes.

Table 20-5. Target Average Rate Index (TARI)

A	Target Contribution	$1,000,000
B	Number of Houses	75
C	Supervisor Hours per House	50
D = (B × C)	Total Hours	3,750
E = (A ÷ D)	Target Average Rate Index (TARI)	$267

He agreed to track hours and contribution over a four-month period and I explained it would come to nothing without a weekly action meeting with the five supervisors.

At the end of the trial period, we met again and reviewed the results (Table 20-6).

Table 20-6. Tracking Contribution and Hours, 4-Month Period Ending _____

Supervisor	Houses	Contract Price ($) A	Contribution ($) B = (A – Cost)	Margin (%) C = (B ÷ A)	Hours D	Average per Hour ($) E = (B ÷ D)
BC	5	650,000	75,000	11.5	260	288
JK	4	540,000	45,000	8.3	250	180
MN	6	780,000	69,000	8.8	367	188
LH	5	630,000	78,000	12.4	245	318
DR	5	640,000	79,000	12.3	254	311
Total	25	3,240,000	346,000	10.7	1,376	251
Target	25		333,750		1,250	267
Variance			+12,250		+126	-16

It was apparent that:

1. Two supervisors were underperforming in comparison with the other three.
2. Three supervisors were taking firmer control over the estimating, purchasing, and construction process.
3. It would be feasible to offer a bonus incentive to supervisors achieving in excess of 11% contribution margin on cost.

4. Targeting 50 hours by a TARI of $267 per house was providing a much-needed focus for the business as a whole.
5. There was a sense of direction and purpose beginning to take hold in the minds of the key players.

Supervisors had viewed their role as that of supervising construction to acceptable levels. Although the length of time to complete a house mattered in the context of achieving a profitable outcome, there was no specific time factor involved other than "let's get it done without too many delays."

With the 50-hours-per-house approach, their individual focus changed from "getting things done" to "how can we best get things done within a time frame of 50 hours?"

The supervisory role changed to that of a building contractor whose bottom line and cash flow[6] depended on maximizing the efficiency and coordinating the input of various sub-trades. In this case, the bottom line was the incentive bonus.

The method proved so effective in gaining control and winning more quotes that the company completed 92 homes in the target year without any increase in staff except for the addition of an assistant estimator. Net profit came in at $340,000.

"Next year," the contractor told me, "we'll do better. I am determined to get the cash flow under control so that we can improve on our purchasing costs. At present we're paying top rates for materials because we can't pay in 30 days, but at least we know the way and how to get there, and that's the main thing."

Under the circumstances, I could only agree.

Case Comment

At the heart of every business, large or small, lies a key driver of activity. There are many drivers and numerous activities, but there is a key driver fundamental to the others.

In this case, it would be reasonable to presume the key driver relates to the number of homes built, but on second thought, we can see the key driver is more connected to control of the building process rather than the house itself, which is the outcome.

---

[6]Cash flow refers to the need to balance the flow of cash payments with the flow of cash receipts.

Assigning a target contribution value per hour to the supervisors recognizes that they are in the driver's seat and accountable for achieving the desired outcome.

Targeting and tracking in this manner focused the attention of management and supervisors on the value of an hour of supervisor time and what was needed to achieve its full potential. The following case study of a hairdressing salon clearly demonstrates that for a business to succeed, technical skill, however brilliant, requires focus on the value of time.

CHAPTER 21

Award-Winning Hairdressing Salon Cuts Its Way Out of Bankruptcy

The national "Hairdresser of the Year" award came at a time when the salon was in danger of closure

Since they started paying employee wages using their own credit cards, the two partners had been deliberating when they should tell their 16 staff and numerous loyal customers there was no alternative but to close the doors.

Struggling to keep the business alive after a sudden collapse of the tourist trade due to a disaster, they had moved to a more fashionable location. The new salon had a basement for shampoo and head massage, a ground floor for

Chapter 21 | Award-Winning Hairdressing Salon Cuts Its Way Out of Bankruptcy

cutting, a first floor for coloring, and a second floor for beauticians' treatment. However, the rent was double that of the previous location.

Anthony, the hairdressing partner and winner of the Hairdresser of the Year Award, attracted top staff and celebrity customers, including models, television and radio stars, senior executives, and leading socialites.

No one looking at the business from outside would have thought that it was experiencing financial difficulties, or that David, the partner in charge of administration, kept up his long-haul flight attendant's role in order to provide cash.

It was through a chance meeting with one of their customers that I met the partners and accepted their invitation to run a health check on the salon.

A 20-minute on-the-spot analysis revealed the salon was charging out an average of $81 per hour for a daily average of 3 hours, 51 minutes per hairdresser (Table 21-1).

Table 21-1. Identifying Average Contribution per Hour[1]

Cash Register Number	Sale Price Net of Tax ($) A	Cost of Materials ($) B	Contribution ($) C = A − B	Hours D	Average Per Hour ($) E = (C ÷ D)
132	160	20	140	2	70
141	90	20	70	1.5	47
159	145	15	130	1.3	100
180	127	7	120	1	120
186	215	25	190	2	95
198	80	15	65	1	65
Total	817	102	715	8.8	81

Given an approximation of an average hourly charge rate,[2] it was possible to get a fix on productivity by referring to the previous year's financials (Table 21-2).

---

[1] Sale price refers to the charge for one hair appointment randomly selected from the cash register; the selection could include more than one appointment for any one staff member.
[2] The charge rate includes contribution from the sale of salon products.

Improving Profit

Table 21-2. Estimating Productivity[3]

A	Contribution[4]	$800,000
B	Average Contribution from Sample	$81[5]
C = (A ÷ B)	Estimated Hours Sold	9,877
D	Hairdresser Hours Paid	18,002
E = (C ÷ D)	Productivity %	55%[6]

Bearing in mind the hairdressers were paid for 8 hours a day, the news came as a shock to both partners, who were under the impression that, if anything, they were understaffed and unable to make appointments for potential clients at the busy times.

Times for appointments were reviewed and the hour allocated to a cut was reduced to 45 minutes. Certain staffers objected strongly, claiming it would not be possible to maintain the high level of service if they had to speed up a cut.

Further investigation revealed the one-hour appointment for a cut included a 15-minute shampoo and head massage treatment undertaken by an apprentice. The hairdresser was in fact waiting for the customer at an empty chair during this time. The actual cut was completed in 45 minutes.

Allowance was made for the initial massage and shampoo by booking the appointment for the customer 15 minutes ahead of the appointment for the hairdresser.

Further revenue erosion was abated when aspiring models were informed that their discounts of 50% would be cut back to 25%—with barely a reduction in business.

Deciding the partners should be averaging closer to $90 an hour, and budgeting for an increase in expenses and profit, we roughed out a target for the year ahead (Table 21-3).

---

[3]Estimating productivity based on using $81 from a random sample can be challenged. For example, "How accurate is the $81?" It does not need to be accurate at this point in time. It simply gets the process of tracking actual results underway, when the true picture will emerge.
[4]*Contribution* is the amount left over to cover expenses and profit, after paying for resale purchases. More often than not referred to as *gross profit*.
[5]Includes contribution from salon product sales.
[6]55% of an 8-hour day = 4 hours and 24 minutes.

Chapter 21 | Award-Winning Hairdressing Salon Cuts Its Way Out of Bankruptcy

Table 21-3. Targeting Performance for the Year Ending _____

A	Target Expenses	$830,000
B	Target Profit	$250,000
C = (A + B)	Target Contribution[7]	$1,080,000
D	Target Average Rate Index (TARI)	$90
E = (C ÷ D)	Target Billable Hours	12,000
F	Hours Paid	18,002
G = (E ÷ F)	Productivity	67%[8]

Tracking daily and weekly performance for comparison with TARI, David, in conjunction with senior staff with whom he shared results, developed an increasingly clear focus on where the rubber met the road.

Taking advantage of Saturday morning staff meetings prior to opening the doors for the day, he introduced Action Sheets (Table 21-4), pinpointing who was to do what by when. The staff entered into the exercise with growing enthusiasm, particularly when they saw their ideas for achieving added value through improved service were taken seriously and acted upon.

Table 21-4. Action Sheet—8/10/xx

Date	Item	Action	Who	When
8/10	Appointments	Allow 15 minutes for wash and head massage	Mary	8/11
8/10	Welcoming	Offer refreshments—tea/coffee/drinks on arrival	Mary / Babs	8/11
8/10	Customer Service	Monitor and report back weekly	Marge	8/17
8/10	Next Meeting			8/17

Present at meeting: MB, BS, MG, KD, DH, NR, TG, KC

Action included nominating one of the senior hairdressers to monitor progress on customer service, which included more meaningful assessment of customer requirements at the time of booking the appointment. Greater

---

[7]Includes contribution from salon product sales.
[8]67% of an 8-hour day = 5 hours 22 minutes.

emphasis was placed on welcoming and friendly support, making use of existing amenities such as tea, coffee, Champagne, or beer for refreshment, as well as three new computers for customers eager to check e-mail or Facebook.

The theme came through loud and clear: "We Care!"

Results after the initial four weeks revealed the salon was achieving an average of $108 at 4 hours, 5 minutes a day per hairdresser. It was a substantial improvement over a TARI of $90, although it fell below the 5-hours, 22-minute target.

Feeling he was finally getting a grip on the business and that a great burden was slowly but surely lifting from his shoulders, David caught fresh enthusiasm. No longer wanting to escape from a depressing financial environment, he applied for and received approval from his airline to take a four-month leave.

Results after eight weeks revealed the salon was achieving an average hourly rate of $119 with an average output per hairdresser of 5 hours a day.

For the first time since the downturn in tourism, the salon made an operational profit for the month, enough to pay wages to the partners and begin to pay down the credit card debt.

Results after 12 weeks showed an operational profit of $17,100 with an average hourly rate of $127.

"I used to walk around the salon and chat with staff and customers," said David, "but I became so worried about the finances and the possibility of closing the doors that I shut myself in the office away from it all. It was too painful to do anything else. Now I can see where we are going."

David elaborated: "TARI gives me focus and the Action Sheets give me the means of making things happen. We used to take minutes at staff meetings and nothing ever happened. I asked our accountant years ago for input on how to improve the business. He only ever said, 'Make more money.' Which, when you come to think of it was the way to go. At least now we know how."

Case Comment

At the outset of my involvement, the business was using popular salon software to record and track appointments and times per staff member along with payments in and out. They relied on their external accountant for the typical account information needed for compiling and filing annual tax returns.

Hourly rates varied from $350 down to $50, and there was a fair degree of discounting—especially for actual or potential celebrities. While there was a general awareness of the time a haircut, shampoo, or coloring should take, there was no follow-through to relate those times with actual times taken by staff.

Chapter 21 | Award-Winning Hairdressing Salon Cuts Its Way Out of Bankruptcy

The salon would appear to be busy all day and all week, but without a means of comparing scheduled or standard times per appointment against actual times, it was not possible to overcome the problem, the symptom of which was falling cash levels.

Once the level of productivity was made known and a TARI established, it became a simple matter of daily and weekly tracking against target to get the salon back on course. In conjunction with weekly feedback on customer service, the reality of being a "caring salon" was reflected in additional appointments and improved productivity.

David considered the Action Sheet a key to the turnaround, because it gave him the means of making things happen so that well-meaning intentions by staff to do this or that could actually be followed through.

Before wrapping up the Case Studies selected for this book, we will look more closely at the Action Sheet as a means of making things happen.

CHAPTER 22

Multi-Department Store Whitewashes the Past

It was hammered home to me that genius might be 20% of an idea, but implementation is 80%. This assignment demonstrated a tried-and-tested technique that made things happen

The client company was a major retailer in the city and had been for the past hundred years. They operated a city store and three suburban stores, employing 64 buyers for 64 departments staffed in turn by 2,000 employees.

As agreed upon between the company and a senior consultant, my assignment was to improve the goods flow throughout the main city store. Goods were offloaded from trucks at the basement Receiving Room from a lane that ran

Chapter 22 | Multi-Department Store Whitewashes the Past

under the building from one busy street to another. It seemed the delay in getting the goods to the departments, spread over four floors, was causing frustration.

While reviewing the problem during my first week, I spoke with several buyers and came across a listing of the daily sales target for each department. Sales for the day were increased by adding a percentage to sales for the same day in the previous year. The increase was said to be due to inflation.

Sales measured in dollars were climbing in the inflationary climate that prevailed, however, masking a problem. During conversations with several buyers, it appeared the number of sales had been falling and, in the absence of any report providing a comparison of numbers for the company as a whole, the matter had continued unnoticed.

Taking time off from the goods-flow traffic, I drew up a simple format and spent an hour or two in the company's office accessing sales volumes and numbers over a two-year period for the 64 departments (Table 22-1).

Table 22-1. Comparison of Sales Volume and Numbers, for 2 Years Ending _____

Department	Year 1		Year 2		Variance	
	Sales ($)	Numbers	Sales ($)	Numbers	Sales ($)	Numbers
Baby Wear	450,000	6,920	470,000	6,120	+20,000	–800
Boys' Wear	380,000	4,470	395,000	4,050	+15,000	–420
China	550,000	4,580	576,000	4,190	+26,000	–390
Girls' Wear	460,000	4,670	468,000	4,260	+8,000	–410
Total for 64 Departments	31,580,000	544,000	33,159,000	512,000	+1,579,000	–32,000

After bringing the problem to the attention of the senior consultant, he persuaded the company to change direction to tackle the unit decline.

I was upgraded to an office next to the patriarch managing director on the fifth floor. It was a freshly painted ex nineteenth-century washroom, furnished with a walnut desk and swivel chair. The building was old and lifts stopped at the fourth floor, encouraging a fair degree of exercise as I went up and down to meet with buyers and work on developing new budgets aimed at increasing the number of sales.

Under threat of serious malformation by my consulting supervisor if I should fail to hold a formal action meeting each week with the managing director and his team of general managers, I complied reluctantly, for it seemed that action was always on me. I created an Action Sheet (Table 22-2) in anticipation of the next meeting.

Table 22-2. Action Sheet Date _____

Date	Item	Action	By Whom	By When
7/09	Budgets	Complete budget for Menswear Department	KC	7/10
7/09	Budgets	Complete budget for Haberdashery Department	KC	7/11
7/09	Budgets	Complete budget for Kitchenware Department	KC	7/11
7/09	Timeline	Schedule a program for completion of all 64 departments	KC	7/15
	Next Meeting			7/18

Present: JJ, GJ, BJ, LJ, KC

After four weeks had passed, and I had prepared budgets for 34 departments with 30 to go, the supervising consultant, who visited once a week and chatted with the management, told me the client was dissatisfied with my progress. In their view, they were paying top dollar to the consulting firm, and they expected to see more for their money.[1]

Although agreeing with my protest that I was flat-out, he said I needed to do something to make them feel they were getting their money's worth while I was still working on the budgets.

When I asked for his suggestions as to what I should do in addition to what I was already doing, he shrugged his shoulders as he hurried away and said, "I'm sure you will work out something."

As I came to work the next day and entered the store via the Receiving Room entrance, I noticed the lane had been blackened with the carbon exhaust, dust, and dirt of the past hundred years. I had been in the lane several times before, but this was the first time I really saw it looking so black and grimy.

At the next action meeting, I decided to bring the matter up by noting "Receiving Room Lane" as an item in the Action Sheet.

After we had dealt with budgets and nominated the departments to be reviewed during the subsequent week, the managing director eyed the lane item (Table 22-3) with raised eyebrows.

---

[1] It was a concern no doubt exacerbated by my having to present the long-serving company secretary with a weekly invoice on behalf of my consulting group for my 40 hours of input. In comparison with his own weekly paycheck, the amount would have been a source of considerable stress. It was also 10 times my own paycheck!

Chapter 22 | Multi-Department Store Whitewashes the Past

Table 22-3. Action Sheet Date: _____

Date	Item	Action	By Whom	By When
8/09	Budgets	Complete Men's Wear	KC	8/10
8/09	Budgets	Complete Boy's Wear	KC	8/12
8/09	Budgets	Complete Cosmetics	KC	8/14
8/09	Receiving Room Lane	Whitewash	GJ	8/15
	Next Meeting			8/16

Present: JJ, GJ, BJ, LJ, KC

There was a long, loud silence as I could hear them thinking: "$XXX a day and he wants to whitewash the lane."

The managing director sighed audibly and looked over his glasses at the director of Store Maintenance. "Will you attend to that, George?"

George looked up from his doodling, a little taken aback at this sudden turn of events. "All right, Dad." His tone was distinctly casual.

"When will you do it, George?" I asked, writing his initials in the By Whom column and poised to add the date.

"Oh, next week I suppose." He watched me inscribe the date accordingly.

During my upstairs-downstairs budgeting activity the following week, I hardly had time to notice what was happening, if anything, in the lane.

At the next meeting, after the budget items were dealt with, we arrived at the item "Receiving Room Lane." There was dead silence as all eyes looked at George. It had not been done and all those present knew it hadn't been done, including George, who was hoping it would go away.

"When will you do it, George?" I asked with pen poised ready to enter the date.

"Oh, next week. Yes, next week" said George.

I carefully noted the date (Table 22-4).

Improving Profit

Table 22-4. Action Sheet Date: _____

Date	Item	Action	By Whom	By When
8/16	Budgets	Complete Children's Wear	KC	8/18
8/16	Budgets	Complete Ladies Wear	KC	8/20
8/16	Budgets	Complete Food Hall	KC	8/22
8/16	Receiving Room Lane	Whitewash	GJ	8/23
	Next Meeting			8/23

Present: JJ, GJ, BJ, LJ, KC

When the matter was raised again the following week, nothing had been done. The MD beamed a steely eye at George.

"What happened, George?" he queried.

"I got caught up with a problem at one of the stores," he said lamely.

"When will you do it, George?" I asked, poised to note the date on the Action Sheet.

His father appeared unusually ruffled as the pressure mounted on George as well as his fellow directors. It was about then that I came to appreciate the value of the Action Sheet.

At the next meeting, the budgets were dealt with as usual. The whitewashing of the lane seemed to stand out more than ever, for we all knew it remained untouched by human hand, and George was conspicuous by his absence.

After 42 years successfully withstanding many an onslaught, George knew from experience that what might seem urgent today, invariably faded in the face of inaction. However, the Receiving Room Lane would not go away and he was at a loss for how to handle it.

The focus on departmental budgets seemed to melt away in light of the more pressing matter of the lane.

I had just arrived at the basement entrance to the store on the Saturday following George's no-show and saw the managing director arrive in his chauffeur-driven Rolls-Royce.

The Rolls glided into the lane and stopped. The chauffeur opened the door and assisted his passenger out of the car before opening the trunk to extract two pots of whitewash along with two large brushes. Opening a pot, he stirred the contents while his passenger struggled into a pair of white overalls.

To my surprise, the 80-year-old managing director, more than ready for action, started sloshing whitewash onto the walls of the lane.

Chapter 22 | Multi-Department Store Whitewashes the Past

Word of what was going on in the lane spread like wildfire throughout the store. Directors, general managers, and store executives appeared from everywhere. Uncertain of the outcome, I discreetly withdrew to the sound of George crying, "Dad! Dad! For goodness' sake!"

On Monday morning, the lane was almost blinding in its whiteness—an extraordinary transformation from its previous state. Employees heading into the lane on their way to clock in at the security entrance were shocked, many thinking they had entered the wrong lane.

I could sense a change of attitude toward me from all the staff, as though they now appreciated I was really worth the money my firm was charging. This was especially so when the General Manager called all the buyers together and informed them I enjoyed the complete confidence of the Board.

For me, it was a revealing insight into the power of the Action Sheet, and I began to use it freely. There were 10 controllers in charge of the 64 buyers and I started weekly action meetings with them, getting agreement on who was going to do what by when.

I encouraged the buyers to have fortnightly meetings with their departments and send me copies of the Action Sheets. However, it was not until staff at the grassroots level realized they could put items on the agenda for discussion and action that they too began to appreciate the value of the exercise. For example, an employee wanting to bring up a matter as simple as a new lock for the staff room toilet door would contact a clerk in the secretary's office to have it noted on the relevant Action Sheet.

In nine months, the company turned the corner and began to pick up on unit volume and gross profit contribution as weekly feedback relating to the number of sales, average sale, and contribution per sale was brought to the notice of staff in each department.

They came to see themselves working together as a team to achieve the desired target, while the Action Sheets provided a vital channel through which communication was maintained and action brought to pass. While awareness of the need to tackle the falling unit volume was vital to the exercise, implementing the changes necessary to bring it about was the key to success.

Two years later, I bumped into James, the National Promotions Manager, in a busy street not far from the store.

"How's it going, James?" I asked.

"Fantastic!" he exclaimed in his happy-go-lucky way. "Fantastic!"

"What do you put the success down to?" I queried.

"No question, no question, at all!" he said, pumping my hand. "Those little sheets you put us on to ... what were they called ... Action Sheets. Yes that's it, Action Sheets!"

He took off as I called out, "Are you still keeping them?"

"No need," he yelled above the noise of passing traffic. "Everything's all right now!"

Case Comment

Important as CBA/TARI is to any business, it is unlikely to groove into the daily routine without a systematic approach to its implementation.

Of all the tools available to management, the Action Sheet has to be rated high on the list. Without it, all the good ideas for improving performance will fall down for lack of a means of implementation.

Seven aspects of the Action Sheet are worth noting:

1. *You must have consensus*. The person nominated for the action must be at the meeting and in agreement.

2. Limit discussion on any item to five minutes at most. For example, an item such as "falling sales" can be dealt with by asking for a report laying out the relevant facts. This approach helps the meeting focus on the first step and avoids the stress of trying to resolve problems at the meeting.

3. Note that the Action Sheet puts a clearer focus on the issues involved. For example, "Bank complaining about slow repayments" may have more to do with collecting accounts receivable, so a discussion about the bank manager could be well off track.

4. Calls for action that fall on "everybody at the meeting" pinpoint nobody in particular and are unlikely to achieve the desired result.

5. Number items according to date, so when they are carried forward it becomes evident how long they have remained on the agenda.

6. Meetings chaired by a senior manager will not necessarily achieve the desired input from less-senior staff. Better to get the staff to conduct the meetings among themselves, with occasional visits by senior management.

7. Staff wishing to place items on the agenda need to be able to do so without fear of repercussion. A neutral staff member should be nominated as a recipient for items.

Chapter 22 | Multi-Department Store Whitewashes the Past

Although this case preceded the crystallization of the concepts underlying CBA and TARI, to the extent that it aimed at increasing the number and contribution value of sales, it was heading in the right direction.

This brings us to the next chapter, in which senior business executives from 14 different businesses examine the relevance of CBA/TARI as applied to their business.

CHAPTER 23

14 Businesses Explore CBA/TARI

Senior executives from companies varying in size from branches of multinationals to small and medium enterprises attended a week-long residential program on the relevance of Contribution-Based Activity for bottom-line improvement.

Highly intrigued, they speculated on how the concepts might be applied to their own circumstances.

They were encouraged to try it for themselves, and if so inclined, to submit their findings, so that others might benefit from the exploration of CBA and TARI.

Although the findings have been summarized for the sake of brevity, they remain faithful to the wording in the transcripts of participants, whose names, along with their companies, have been changed to ensure confidentiality.

Unless otherwise stated, the variety of currencies involved have been approximated to their value in US dollars.

23.1 Vehicle Manufacturing

Bill Jones is on the management team in the production division of Company M, which manufactures vehicles for domestic and export markets. As a first step in applying the CBA/TARI concepts he has learned about, he decides to carry out an invoice analysis of the best-selling vehicles (Table 23.1-1).[1]

Table 23.1-1. Invoice Analysis

Number	Invoice Price per Vehicle ($) A	Materials at Cost Price ($) B	Gross Profit Contribution ($) C = (A − B)	Gross Profit (%) D = (C ÷ A)	Number of Production-Hours E	Average Gross Profit per Production-Hour ($) F = (C ÷ E)
1	31,480	24,500	6,980	22	32	218
2	10,250	7,250	3,000	29	24	125
3	8,700	6,246	2,454	28	22	112
4	12,800	9,344	3,456	27	26	133
5	6,700	4,824	1,876	28	19	99
Total	69,930	52,164	17,766	25	123	144

"I noted the invoice analysis revealed interesting variations, with gross profit [GP] percentage ranging from 22% to 29%. Seeing I had assumed the GP would be much the same, this was a bit of a surprise!

"Recalling the suggestion that we should look ahead and push the boundaries a bit, reducing the cost of materials by 5%, I projected a scenario where the products sold at an average gross profit contribution margin of 29%, with marginally fewer hours for manufacture (see Table 23.1-2).

---

[1] Invoice and material prices are net of tax.

Improving Profit

Table 23.1-2. Invoice Analysis Assuming an Average GP of 29% and Marginally Fewer Hours to Manufacture

Number	Invoice Price (Net of Tax) ($) A	Materials at Cost Price (Net of Tax) ($) B	Gross Profit Contribution ($) C = (A − B)	Gross Profit (%) D = (C ÷ A)	Number of Production-Hours E	Average Gross Profit per Production-Hour ($) F = (C ÷ E)
1	31,480	23,275	8,205	26	30	273
2	10,250	6,887	3,363	33	23	146
3	8,700	5,934	2,766	32	21	132
4	12,800	8,877	3,923	31	25	157
5	6,700	4,582	2,118	32	18	118
Total	69,930	49,555	20,375	29	117	174

"The average increase in gross profit contribution of close to $522 per vehicle[2] with an output of 200,000 vehicles would mean an additional contribution exceeding $100 million (200,000 × $522 = $104,400,000). Improving efficiency by achieving a 5% reduction in the number of production hours would potentially improve output by 10,000 cars (200,000 + 5% = 210,000), boosting contribution by a further $40 million depending on the product mix.[3]

Table 23.1-3. Identifying Average Increase in Contribution

A	Contribution, Table 23-1	$17,766.00
B	Contribution, Table 23-2	$20,375.00
C = (B − A)	Increase in Contribution of 5 Vehicles	$2,609.00
D = (C ÷ 5)	Average Increase per Vehicle	$521.80
E	Production-Hours, Table 23-1	123
F	Production-Hours, Table 23-2	117
G = (F ÷ E)	Improved Efficiency (117 + 5% = 123)	5%

"I know it must look a bit like pie in the sky," Bill wrote, "but it is the first time I have been able to get a clear look at the whole picture. Whenever I want to get information, I only need to access the software and ask the question to get a ream of data. But that is the problem; it doesn't give me a simple overview.

---

[2]($20,375 − $17,766) = ($2,609 ÷ 5) = $522.
[3]Average GP per vehicle ($20,375 ÷ 5) = $4,075. ($4,075 × 10,000) = $40,750,000.

"In the time available to date, I have not been able to obtain estimates of the cost of implementing such an invoice analysis and tracking procedure, but whatever the cost, it is necessary to help focus attention on such key information."

23.2 Manufacturing and Distribution

John Smith is assistant chief finance officer of Company Y, which is involved in manufacturing and trading. The manufacturing company sells products to the trading company, and the latter sells them to distributors.

Analysis of Invoices: Results and Potential Utility

"Approximately 200+ invoices to customers are issued monthly, with every invoice including from 20 to 40 lines (different products in different quantities). For the analysis, I took 10 invoices. The sample (Table 23.2-1) was chosen randomly, but in such a manner that would include sales to different types of customers in different regions (urban and rural).

Table 23.2-1. Invoice Analysis

Number	Invoice Price (Net of Tax) ($)	Goods at Cost Price ($)	Gross Profit Contribution ($)	Gross Profit Contribution (%)
1	67,901	51,342	16,559	24.4
2	11,804	8,180	3,624	30.7
3	68,982	49,587	19,395	28.1
4	4,753	3,936	817	17.2
5	47,940	34,084	13,856	28.9
6	30,165	24,279	5,886	19.5
7	3,475	2,517	958	27.6
8	12,063	8,997	3,066	25.4
9	5,448	4,423	1,025	18.8
10	30,093	21,840	8,253	27.4
Total	282,624	209,185	73,439	26.0

"The average sale of the sample, $28,264 ($282,624 ÷ 10), multiplied by the number of invoices for the period, is within 4% of actual sales for the same period and proves the sample is representative.

"The analysis shows significant spread of gross profit, depending on the distributor. To determine a clear trend, more detailed analysis is required; however, even this small sample highlights the most profitable and the least profitable of the distributors, depending largely on their location.

"However, this analysis shows weak areas that should be addressed. Taking into account that the least profitable distributor for the company is also the most expensive in terms of delivery, the sales force should be oriented on improving customer orders in terms of portfolio mix; the task directly related to this is to increase demand in retail.

"My recommendation is to set a gross-profit-contribution target margin per invoice for sales force and measure their performance according to this target. I would recommend upgrading the existing system so that it would be able to generate such reports on a regular basis. Technically it is possible, as all necessary data are already contained in the system. Monitoring average gross profit per item as well as per invoice will be a valuable tool for sales managers, allowing them to identify problematic distributors/retail customers. It can also be an instrument of measuring performance of sales force.

"This analysis, conducted on a regular basis, should help the company to achieve improvement of portfolio mix that was recommended in previous reports."

Conclusion and Recommendations

"I found the cost system of the company adequate and ensuring correct calculation of product costs. As regards the management information system, it needs improvement directed on integration of different sources of data into a single system and decreasing manual workload. This issue needs to be addressed to the IT department.

"I also recommend carrying out invoices analysis (namely calculating average gross profit per invoice and per item) on a regular basis through automated process in the accounting system. This analysis should serve as a basis for improving portfolio mix."

23.3 Distribution

Mary Southend is the Accounts manager of Company Z, engaged in large-scale distribution.

Manual Analysis

"I'm going to carry out manual analysis of the customer's invoices for one month. This timeline was selected because of the large amount of invoices during a year. This sampling should represent the company's sales. For representation of the overall picture, I decided to include at least three invoices from each sales division (Table 23.3-1).

Table 23.3-1. Invoice Analysis

Number	Invoice Price (Net of Tax) ($) A	Goods or Materials at Cost Price ($) B	Gross Profit ($) C = (A − B)	Gross Profit (%) D = (C ÷ A)
Region A				
1	59,438	44,587	14,851	24.98
2	58,908	44,757	14,151	24.02
3	16,713	11,896	4,817	28.82
Region B				
4	41,581	28,403	13,178	31.69
5	29,154	21,864	7,290	25.00
6	40,829	28,913	11,916	29.19
7	67,901	51,034	16,867	24.84
Region C				
8	15,170	11,720	3,450	22.74
9	41,748	30,219	11,529	27.61
10	34,750	25,177	9,573	27.55
Total	**406,192**	**298,570**	**107,622**	**26.50**

"To check that samples are representative, total gross profit contribution for the period was divided by the average gross profit per sale. The result is close to the genuine number of sales that were made in that month. The sample highlights the distributor with the highest average gross profit, as well the distributor with the lowest.

"The account system currently being used, if upgraded to the CBA system, will seriously improve the allocation of overheads, taking account of the distribution expenses related to high and low performers.

"Moreover, implementation of an invoice analysis review on a regular basis could assist in focusing management's attention on roots of possible performance limiters as well as acting as basis for internal benchmarking tool between sales divisions."

Note It is important to remember that a shift from the traditional system calls for education of personnel and will take time.

Conclusion and Recommendations

"Without accurate allocation of overheads relating to distribution, it is a hopeless task trying to determine a product's profitability. Classical accounting systems do not reflect real cost consumption and therefore represent distorted information used by management for development of tactical and strategic decisions. The cost of mistakes is high.

"It is necessary to upgrade the current system. In a market showing little growth, when a company cannot sell more than market can consume, contribution-based activity accounting becomes essential to sustaining a competitive advantage. Taking into account the low cost of implementation and absence of serious changes in user's interface, the upgrade can be implemented less than in six months. Moreover, cost of upgrade includes incorporation of the production and sales departments into the financial system. At the second stage of the project it is possible to introduce benchmarking tools based on the invoice analysis."

23.4 Software Development

Sam Betts heads up the support team of XYZ, a branch of a multinational software development and outsourcing company focused on delivering quality, cost-effective software solutions.

"My branch of the company is primarily involved in marketing and supporting products as well as upgrading and developing progams. I carried a sample invoice analysis" (Table 23.4-1).

Table 23.4-1. Sample Invoice Analysis

Number	Invoice Price ($) A	Cost Price ($) B	Gross Profit ($) C = (A − B)	Gross Profit % D = (C ÷ A)	Hours E	Average Gross Profit per Hour ($) F = (C ÷ E)
1	12,880	9,600	3,280	25.5	55	60
2	24,760	17,720	7,040	28.4	88	80
3	8,640	8,460	180	2.1	48	4
4	3,020	3,175	155	−5	15	−10
5	14,000	12,600	1,400	10	56	25
6	6,000	6,140	140	−2.3	30	−5
7	15,680	10,580	5,100	32.5	78	65
8	8,540	7,890	650	7.6	47	14
9	10,400	9,600	800	7.7	52	15
10	12,880	10,240	2,640	20.5	71	37
Total	116,800	96,005	20,795	17.8	540	38.5

"The range of gross profit per item is quite significant. Older agreements with fixed rates yield lower gross profit in comparison with newer agreements where higher rates were negotiated.

"Some jobs even result in negative gross profit, which reveals that some urgent steps must be taken to bring them back to path of profitability. Rate increases, lower expenses, and better control over overhead will help to achieve better financial results on projects.

"Based on the results of the analysis, it can be observed that there are inaccurate results from current manual reporting processes. To solve this problem, the company should invest in a new software system that will connect all pieces of information together and allow it to get more informative and timely management accounting reports."

Conclusion and Recommendations

"XYZ's pricing and productivity is based on a billed consulting hour. The hours are reported by employees via a time tracking system, then manually transferred to Excel spreadsheets, and along with other expense and revenues they are used in developing charge rate formulas.

"Based on the analysis results, it is clear that three cornerstone pieces of information—actual reported time, expenditures, and revenues—will participate in generation of the management reports. All three will have to be connected via software system, eliminating risk of human error, and allowing timely access to the reports. This will make the profitability calculation easy and transparent not only to top management but also to department managers.

"The analysis also revealed that some projects are not performing well, and actions will have to be taken to bring their financial results back on track.

"Overall, the process should be more streamlined and automated whenever possible. The expense for implementation of such a software system will be more than justified."

23.5 Engineering and Design

Jan Jensen is the CEO of ABZ Company, which provides detailed engineering and design services for the mega-construction industry.

"ABZ provides its clients with high-quality technical documentation developed in the Nupas-Cadmatic CAD/CAM system. The fixed price for each project is calculated on the basis of estimated man-hours multiplied by ABZ's hourly rate. Thus, sales are measured in hours. The demand is very high; ABZ literally may sell as much as it produces (subject to quality). Market conditions are favorable, so ABZ may slowly but steady increase its sales tariff. Therefore the strategic goal of ABZ is continuous growth.

"Engineering capacity is computed based on the average 'effective working hours' per engineer."

Analysis of 10 Invoices

"The results of a manual analysis of 10 representative invoices are found in Table 23.5-1.

Table 23.5-1. Invoice Analysis

Number	Invoice Price (Net of Tax) ($) A	Cost Price (Net of Tax) ($) B	Gross Profit ($) C = (A − B)	Gross Profit (%) D = (C ÷ A × 100%)	Number of Hours E	Average Gross Profit per Hour ($) F = (C ÷ E)
1	11,250	8,228	3,022	27	50	60
2	37,125	22,899	14,226	38	165	86
3	149,400	107,682	41,718	28	664	63
4	88,650	63,291	25,359	29	394	64
5	7,192	4,430	2,762	38	23	120
6	3,645	2,310	1,335	37	16	83
7	10,800	7,844	2,956	27	48	62
8	21,976	11,514	10,462	48	107	98
9	10,350	5,696	4,654	45	46	101
10	4,410	2,532	1,878	43	19	99
Total	344,798	236,426	108,372	31	1,532	71

"The average gross profit calculated from the representative invoices is 31%. Apart from giving a close approximation of the average gross profit per hour—approximately $71—the sample also revealed a wide range of contributions per project. It varies from 27% to 48%, which indicates different levels of profitability provided by different projects."

Average Gross Profit and Gross Profit per Man-Hour Comparison

"Dividing the total gross profit of the company for the past year by average gross profit per production-hour, I received a result that is not very close to the actual number of hours sold. However, I would not doubt that the sample of 10 invoices is representative. This discrepancy was most likely caused by a transition of business where the man-hour allocation to the projects was disturbed. Otherwise the comparison of total hours sold versus total actual production hours in this example proved that they are very close."

Comparison of Total Hours Sold vs. Actual Production-Hours Paid

"A further comparison of total hours sold versus total actual production-hours billed showed a variance of 4% to the benefit of the first. ABZ has spent a lot of man-hours for training of personnel additional to the budget, which included a cost for trainers, study material, and travel (when activities were held outside ABZ premises). So in light of these facts, ABZ productivity was relatively high.

"I will now be more considerate toward gross profit contribution values, whereas previously, I have just reduced 'net sales' by 'cost of goods sold,' not thinking of what cost was included! Moreover, I would also review actual versus potential outputs differently. With time, ABZ will be able to collect more statistical data for such analysis, which I think shall be considered when making appraisal of company performance.

"With regard to financial planning, I would approach development of pro forma statements differently. Instead of projecting increase of sales in money terms, I would adopt the target average rate per hour system,[4] which allows balancing prices and expenses much more effectively.

"The most valuable advantage of the financial plan developed using an hourly tariff framework would be the possibility of using it for managerial control of planned values. It could be used for internal benchmarking as well."

Need for Purchase of New Software

"Reforming the existing reporting system will be impossible without IT support. Thus, ABZ management shall consider purchase of a suitable package that would dramatically enrich ABZ organizational capital and improve planning, controlling, and accounting processes.

"It will provide timely and reliable information to all users and particularly to the accounting department, which in turn will provide top management with information crucial for decision making."

23.6 Property: Real Estate

Jeremy Cantrell is CEO of GGD Inc., a corporation founded with the sole purpose of holding and managing residential real estate properties.

---

[4] The reference "target rate per hour system" is to "target average rate index," or "TARI" for short, which combines the key activity driver—in this case, man-hours—with is linked to the target average gross profit contribution per man-hour.

Chapter 23 | 14 Businesses Explore CBA/TARI

"Until present day, the company has no staff besides the owners of the company. The directors feel that it is more economically viable to outsource activities such as accounting, tax preparation, and janitorial/maintenance tasks that occur every year.

"Presently, the company maintains three properties that have been acquired since inception. For the purpose of this report, the previous two years are going to be taken into consideration; thus statistics are available only for two out of the three properties."

Invoice Analysis

"As mentioned, the business in question doesn't produce invoices, and income is being paid directly as a result of executed lease; moreover, the amount of income received every month is exactly the same.

"Table 23.6-1 analyzes the last 10 rents paid and the number of square feet of space being rented.

Table 23.6-1. Invoice Analysis

Number	Invoice Price	Cost price	Gross profit	GP%	No. of sales	Avg. GP per sale	No. of items	Avg. GP per item	No of SQFT	Avg GP per SQFT
1	$900.00	$1,077.00	$(177.00)	-19.67	1	$(177.00)	1	$(177.00)	500	$(0.35)
2	$1,445.00	$841.00	$604.00	41.80	1	$604.00	1	$604.00	840	$0.72
3	$900.00	$1,077.00	$(177.00)	-19.67	1	$(177.00)	1	$(177.00)	500	$(0.35)
4	$1,445.00	$841.00	$604.00	41.80	1	$604.00	1	$604.00	840	$0.72
5	$900.00	$1,077.00	$(177.00)	-19.67	1	$(177.00)	1	$(177.00)	500	$(0.35)
6	$1,445.00	$841.00	$604.00	41.80	1	$604.00	1	$604.00	840	$0.72
7	$900.00	$1,077.00	$(177.00)	-19.67	1	$(177.00)	1	$(177.00)	500	$(0.35)
8	$1,445.00	$841.00	$604.00	41.80	1	$604.00	1	$604.00	840	$0.72
9	$900.00	$1,077.00	$(177.00)	-19.67	1	$(177.00)	1	$(177.00)	500	$(0.35)
10	$1,445.00	$841.00	$604.00	41.80	1	$604.00	1	$604.00	840	$0.72
Total	$11,725.00	$9,590.00	$2,135.00	11.07	1	$2,135.00	10	$213.50	6700	$0.1825

"In the table, cost price included real estate taxes, condominium assessment, and mortgage interest for each individual property, all taken from the Profit and Loss Report figures. Total gross profit contribution posted for the year was $5,130, and total sales revenue made that year was posted as $28,140.

"Dividing the total gross profit by the average gross profit contribution per square foot[5] came to $0.1825 (Table 23.6-2).

Table 23.6-2. Reliability Check of Invoice Sample

A	Total Gross Profit Contribution	$5,130
B	Sample Average Contribution per Square Foot	$0.1825
C = (A ÷ B)	Calculated Space Rented	28,110 sq. ft.
D	Actual Space Rented	28,140 sq. ft.

"The sample very closely matches the total space rented of 28,140 square feet! What's interesting is that the table reveals the gross profit per square foot of space for each individual property, showing that despite the small profitability of the entire business, one of the units is actually not profitable at all, and even considering the probability of modest appreciation of the price on the real estate market, it's losing about $2,124 a year!

"This means that cost of sales (real estate taxes, condominium assessment, and mortgage interest) is greater than the rent moneys it brings in. For it to become profitable, given the current expense levels, it must bring a rent greater than cost of sales each month—at least $1,077.

"This analysis is an eye-opening view into the profit of each individual contributing real-estate asset. The analysis gives a drilled-down picture of what the business consists of. At the end of the day, it's visible that the company is in the business of obtaining revenue from renting square feet of space, which is the ultimate atomic unit; knowing the average gross profit contribution per square foot, it's much easier and clearer to calculate total revenue that the business can achieve if changes are made.

"All of the above figures should ideally have been visible from day one of operations, but it was not clear in our minds what was needed; and in any case, our existing software would not have been able to produce the goods. Now that we know what we are looking for, inquiries so far have not proved fruitful."

---

[5]The average gross profit contribution when applied as a target benchmark is referred to as "Target Average Rate Index" or "TARI."

23.7 Packaging: Production and Distribution

Ray Spence is the financial director of STB Company, producing packaging and goods for everyday use.

"Sixty percent of the goods sold are locally produced, and the 40% balance of goods are imported. Main customers include food producers who need packaging (business to business), wholesale distributors, and key retail accounts."

Invoices Analysis and Comments on Received Results

"In our financial plan, there are 954,000 pieces of goods with $0.45 as average Gross Profit per piece. Assuming 50 weeks, the average number per week will be 19,080 pieces and the average weekly gross profit contribution $8,586.

"We are taking $0.45 as our Target Average Rate Index or TARI as a benchmark. I completed a manual analysis of 10 invoices (Table 23.7-1). These 10 invoices represent one week of invoices, which makes the picture even clearer."

Table 23.7-1. Invoice Analysis of Output for One Week

Number	Invoice Price ($) A	Invoice Cost ($) B	Gross Profit ($) C = (A − B)	Gross Profit (%) D = (C ÷ A)	Number of Sales per Week E	Number of Items per Invoice F	Average Gross Profit per Item ($) G = (C ÷ F)	+/− TARI per Item $0.45
1	7,000	6,380	620	9	1	2,500	0.25	−0.20
2	7,000	6,380	620	9	1	2,500	0.25	−0.20
3	14,000	12,750	1,250	9	1	5,000	0.25	−0.20
4	1,400	1,280	120	9	1	500	0.24	−0.21
5	16,000	12,750	3,250	20	1	5,000	0.65	+0.20
6	6,400	5,100	1,300	20	1	2,000	0.65	+0.20
7	1,700	1,280	420	25	1	500	0.84	+0.39
8	1,700	1,280	420	25	1	500	0.84	+0.39
9	1,700	1,280	420	25	1	500	0.84	+0.39
10	6,000	5,100	900	15	1	2,000	0.45	0
Total	62,900	53,580	9,320	14.8	10	21,000	0.44	−0.01

"The analysis indicates the following:

- "Gross profit contribution per week is higher than planned, which is the result of increasing of sales per week (21,000 pieces instead of planned 19,000 pieces).
- "Gross Profit % per item is almost on the target level 15%, one of the most important indicators for us.
- "Average Gross Profit per item is almost on the target level of $0.45 per item, which is a prime indicator for us and one we would like to control.
- "Analysis of gross profit per piece per separate customer can be compared on a weekly and accumulative basis with TARI as in Table 23.7-2."

Table 23.7-2. Weekly Report

Number	Invoice Price ($) A	Invoice Cost ($) B	Gross Profit ($) C = (A − B)	+/− TARI 8,568 ($) D = (C − TARI)	Gross Profit (%) E = (D ÷ A)	Number of Items per Week F	Average Gross Profit ($) per Item G = (D ÷ F)	+/− TARI per Item $0.45
Total	62,900	53,580	9,320	+752	14.8	21,000	0.44	−0.01

"The total results per week give management an opportunity to check the gross profit contribution per week with target as well as the gross profit contribution per item with the target. We are also able to check the number of items sold, as this also has to be controlled.

"This report has to be accepted by our company to make it easy for management to focus on what really matters. This is valid in cooperation with well-controlled inventory and receivables levels, for purposes of ensuring adequate cash flow.

"By upgrading existing software, we can do this report. That is actually the advantage of this report—simplicity and transparency. Going further in our conclusion and recommendations, we have to focus on efficiency and control.

"Control means:

- "Invoice analysis on weekly and accumulative basis to check actual versus target
- "Slow-moving order dispatch report on weekly basis
- "Expense control on monthly basis"

23.8 Banking

Jill Maison is the chief accountant at XXX Bank, which provides customers with a full range of the most up-to-date commercial products and services.

She commences with a sample analysis of 10 loans (Table 23.8-1).

Table 23.8-1. Analysis of 10 Loans

Number	Loan ($) A	Term in Months B	Cost of Funds + Provision (%) C	Interest Rate (%) D	Total Interest Payment per Year ($) E = (A x D)	Total Cost per Year ($) F	Gross Profit Per Year ($) G = (E − F)	Gross Profit (%) H = (G ÷ E)
1	1,900	24	18.0	65.0	1,235	402	833	67.4
2	2,100	12	18.0	65.0		2,598	−2,598	
3	2,400	36	18.0	65.0	1,560	472	1,088	69.7
4	2,700	24	18.0	65.0	1,755	546	1,209	68.9
5	1,600	24	18.0	65.0	1,040	348	692	66.5
6	2,100	36	18.0	65.0	1,365	418	947	69.4
7	1,600	12	18.0	65.0	1,040	408	632	60.8
8	1,900	12	18.0	65.0	1,235	462	773	62.6
9	2,100	36	18.0	65.0	1,365	418	947	69.4
10	1,600	24	18.0	65.0	1,040	348	692	66.5
Total	20,000		18.0	65.0	11,635	6,420	5,215	44.8

Loan #2 was not paid off by customer because of fraud. That's why the loan amount was added to the total cost. Table 23.8-2 shows the sample is representative.

Table 23.8-2. Representativeness of the Invoices

A	Total Gross Profit Forecast for 12 Months	$12,210,850
B = ($5,215 ÷ 10)	Average Gross Profit from Sample	$522
C = (A ÷ B)	Calculated Number of Loans	23,392
D	Actual Number of Loans Forecast	23,820

Results of the Analysis

"The numbers are very close, meaning that these 10 invoices are representative. The total number of loans revealed from this analysis (23,392) gives us an opportunity to compare it with the budgeted sales amount (23,820). In case of deviation, we may react quickly in advance to improve the situation before the end of the year.

"This analysis could be very helpful since it is an additional tool for evaluating the gross profit margin for every customer/loan. It could also be useful for defining groups of customers with different profitability. Then I could select customers with small or even negative profitability and at the end increase overall profit margin.

"Such analysis on the customer level is not possible to conduct manually because the bank has hundreds of thousands of customers. Information about the loans, customers, and costs is spread among several operating systems used in the bank. These systems are not connected with each other, and the data is in different formats. The only solution is to implement special software."

23.9 Banking

Alex Brendon heads up the Risk Management Department at YYY Bank. As a commercial bank, it is very proactive in its services for individuals and legal entities, especially in lending, and offers a full range of banking products.

"In Table 23.9-1, I analyze the profitability of 10 loan contracts and compare the reliability of the sample with actual figures from the past year."

Table 23.9-1. Profitability Analysis of 10 Loan Contracts

Number/Business	Amount of Credit Agreement, Thousands ($) A	Interest Rate (Annual), % B	Cost of Funds (Annual), % C	Margin (%) B−C	Interest Income per Year, Thousands ($) D = A × B	Interest Expenses per Year, Thousands ($) E = A × C	Gross Profit (Net Interest Income) per Year, Thousands ($) F = D − E	Gross Profit (Net Interest Income), % G = F ÷ D
1/Corporate	2,000	14.0	6.7	7.3	280	134	146	5.10
2/Corporate	1,400	14.5	6.7	7.8	203	94	109	5.38
3/Corporate	3,000	14.0	6.7	7.3	420	201	219	5.21
4/Corporate	5,600	13.5	6.7	6.8	756	375	381	5.04
5/Retail	15.5	17.0	10.7	6.3	2.6	1.3	1.3	4.88
6/Retail	20	17.0	10.7	6.3	3.4	1.7	1.7	4.88
7/Retail	9	17.5	10.7	6.8	1.6	0.8	0.8	5.03
8/Retail	12.5	17.0	10.7	6.3	2.1	1.1	1.0	4.88
9/Retail	34.5	16.5	10.7	5.8	5.7	3.0	2.7	4.73
10/Retail	10^6	17.0	10.7	6.3	1.7	0.9	0.8	4.88
Total	12,101.5				1,676	812	864	5.15

[6]Explanation using 10/Retail, 10.0 = 10,000 loan agreements, with a gross profit of $0.8 per 1000 agreements (10,000 × 0.8) = $8,000 gross profit in total.

"Multiplying the net interest in the sample by the number of loans for the month of October, the net interest income will be $27,771,000. This is very close to the actual net interest income earned in October of $28,394,000.

"This analysis confirms the need to revisit our plans and restructure business processes in order to gain target margin and profitability."

Contribution-Based Activity System and Application of Target Average Rate Index in the Bank

"Applying the Contribution-Based Activity (CBA) system to the financial plan for the year ahead, it is possible to develop a Target Average Rate Index (TARI) per $1,000 loan that could be considered by the bank's management as a benchmark and taken into consideration in assessing performance.

"Following this calculation, the interest rate for every credit agreement must be set at the level that at least contributes to the bank's profit not less than the TARI benchmark.

"In order to implement appropriate analysis of credit agreements and control their contribution to the Bank's profit, it is necessary to upgrade the existing software. The software program should calculate contribution of each credit agreement and make a comparison with the TARI. If the contribution is below TARI, the program must refer to management for confirmation or change of conditions for the loan."

23.10 Automobile Distribution

Nigel Smith is the CEO of ZZZ Car Sales, a large dealership involved with sales and after-sales service of new and used cars.

"The invoice analysis (Table 23.10-1) focuses on the sale of one brand of vehicle based on data drawn from a daily sales report."

Table 23.10-1. Invoice Analysis of "ZZZ" Sales

Number	Sales ($) A	Cost ($) B	Gross Profit Actual ($) C = (A − B)	Gross Profit (%) D = (C ÷ A)	Discount ($)	Days in Stock	Bank Interest ($)
1	84,325	85,700	1,375	1.63	−11,655	505	29,643
2	107,823	99,060	8,763	8.13	−3,127	496	33,653
3	44,073	43,023	1,050	2.38	−1,997	51	1,503
4	125,721	113,280	12,441	0.99	−1,159	52	4,035
5	104,959	99,060	5,899	5.62	−5,991	24	1,628
6	105,063	99,060	6,003	5.71	−5,887	64	4,342
7	81,897	77,110	4,787	5.84	−2,533	7	370
8	82,500	77,110	5,390	6.53	−1,930	57	3,010
9	77,779	71,352	6,426	8.26	−321	10	489
10	88,233	81,701	6,532	7.40	−1,217	1	56
Total	902,373	846,456	55,917	6.20	−35,817		78,729

"In analyzing 10 invoices, I discovered the average gross profit margin of 10 sales is 6.61%. On a daily basis, the salesperson has no financial information in the daily sales report, so I have included the column (bank interest) to show the interest payment for loan money calculated from the quantity of days in stock per car at a bank interest rate of 25% per year.

"The income of the sales department is negative when you take account of the bank interest being $78,729 compared with the gross profit of $55,917. On a daily basis, unaware of bank interest, the salesperson gives a discount to customers.

"If we divide $743,670, the total gross profit of the selected brand, by the average gross profit per sale from the invoice analysis (743,670 ÷ 5,592), we see that 133 units were assumed to be sold during the year. I can say that the sample of 10 invoices was representative, because the sales were 145 units.

"The 10 invoices show the levels of discounts are very wide and illogical. The best way to keep control of GP is to implement the process of weekly monitoring. First, it is necessary to determine the targeted level of gross profit per unit and provide weekly comparison of the result, providing early alert for relevant and timely correction.

"Establishing a target average gross profit contribution as a benchmark for the sales department would be a significant step forward. It would make a weekly appraisal of performance straightforward and simple."

23.11 Household Equipment

Steve Crane is the marketing manager of VVV company, which imports, warehouses, and distributes household equipment.

Table 23.11-1 samples 10 typical invoices.

Table 23.11-1. Invoice Analysis

Number	Invoice Price (Net of Tax) ($) A	Goods at Cost (Net of Tax) ($) B	Gross Profit ($) C = (A − B)	Gross Profit (%) D = (C ÷ A)	Number of Items E	Average Gross Profit per Item ($) C ÷ E
1	142.30	85.51	56.87	39.91	3	18.95
2	453.48	307.01	146.47	32.30	22	6.65
3	182.88	111.90	70.93	38.81	5	14.18
4	89.33	55.35	33.98	38.04	3	11.33
5	633.13	429.19	203.94	32.21	33	6.17
6	108.41	67.96	40.45	37.31	3	13.47
7	241.00	183.48	57.52	23.87	23	2.50
8	154.00	120.91	33.09	21.49	15	2.26
9	187.50	143.90	43.60	23.25	17	2.56
10	500.40	366.73	133.67	26.71	35	3.82
Total	2,692.43	1,871.94	820.49	30.47	159	5.16

"To be sure that our extracts are representative, I divided the total gross profit for the last year by the average gross profit per sale:

"Gross profit ÷ Average gross profit per item = 308,470 ÷ 5.16 = 59,781 pieces.

"We sold 59,910 pieces last year. That means that illustrated invoices are really representative.

"This analysis helps us to control the gross profit received from every sold item to the planned average gross profit. The gross profit per invoice identifies the priority of the sales strategy by indicating which segments are most profitable for the company.

"There is additional useful information in the table. If we divide total gross profit by average gross profit per invoice, we will have the total quantity of transactions made:

"Gross profit $308,470 ÷ ($820.49 ÷ 10) = 3,759 invoices.

"This result is close to the actual figure, and thus we once again confirm that our extracts are representative. From this analysis we can approximate how many invoices we can expect in the following year in accordance with a planned profit level. That allows us to estimate expenses connected with order processing. Thus, we could use this information as part of the process of financial planning.

"As we have seen, the proposed reports could be very useful for the decision-making process, financial planning, and other activities in the company. It should be also very evident that preparing these reports does not involve a lot of time.

"An upgrade of our primary software system will reduce the working hours required for order processing and report preparation, resulting in an increase in total productivity without the need for additional personnel expense.

"The sales force can then strive to achieve planned gross sales, of course, but they can also use the planned average gross profit per sale (TARI) to guide them.

"Comparing results with TARI helps us identify which products are the most profitable and which clients bring most profit to company. This will help our sales force to identify products and clients segments on which they have to focus their attention. In consequence, we could achieve the highest results."

23.12 Specialized Farming Equipment

Marianne Angostini is the CEO of NNN company, which distributes, installs, and services technological equipment for farms involved in specialized planting and harvesting. It purchases, distributes, and installs products from different international suppliers.

Marianne commences with an invoice analysis of the key products (Table 23.12-1).

Chapter 23 | 14 Businesses Explore CBA/TARI

Table 23.12-1. Invoice Analysis

Products	Invoice Price (Net of Tax) ($) A	Cost Price (Net of Tax) ($) B	Gross Profit ($) C = (A − B)	Gross Profit (%) D = (C ÷ A)	Number of Items, Pieces E	Average Gross Profit per Item ($) C ÷ E
A	120,000.00	102,000.00	18,000.00	15	1	18,000
B	3,900.00	2,735.00	1,165.00	30	1	1,165
C	6,800.00	5,440.00	1,360.00	20	1	1,360
D	605.00	242.00	363.00	60	160	2.27
E	516.00	258.00	258.00	50	14	18.43
F	43.90	35.12	8.78	20	13	0.67
I	222.57	178.05	44.52	20	1	44.52
J	224.08	168.06	56.02	25	4	14.00
K	200.00	160.00	40.00	20	2	20.00
L	514.00	411.20	102.80	20	33	3.11
Total	133,025.55	111,627.43	21,398.12	16.09	230	93.03

"The calculation of gross profit margin from 10 analyzed invoices resulted in 16.09%, which is close to the company's overall gross profit of 17%. It indicates the sample of 10 invoices was representative.

"The analysis shows that it is most profitable for the company to sell product C, as its cost price is not high, the time needed for installation is low (2–4 days, in comparison to 35–60 days for Product A), and the number of technicians required is not labor intensive.[7]

"Also the demand for product C is quite stable and in certain times of the year is very high. To illustrate, let's take an example. We can sell 13 of product C to receive the same gross profit of 1 product A. But to sell 1 product A, we need to spend much more time than we do to sell product C.

"As for improvements in software, I can see that an upgrade will help the company to significantly improve gross profit performance, compared with the system now in use."

---

[7] The reasoning for preferring C relates to greater frequency of demand compared with A and B, less time to install, and (in the case of A) less strain on the cash flow.

23.13 Importing and Distributing

Michael Howe is the marketing manager for JKL, a company importing and distributing products to the final customers through a dealer network.

Table 23.13-1 shows an invoice analysis for the company's three main directions: (1) consumer products, (2) professional products, and (3) spare parts.

Consumer Products

Table 23.13-1. Invoice Analysis: Sales of Consumer Goods

Number	Invoice Price ($) A	Goods or Materials at Cost Price ($) B	Gross Profit ($) C = (A − B)	Gross Profit (%) D = (C ÷ A)	Number of Items E	Average Gross Profit per Item ($) F = (C ÷ E)
1	560.00	448.00	112.00	20	3	37.33
2	1,020.00	856.80	163.20	16	5	32.64
3	940.00	761.40	178.60	19	4	44.65
4	870.00	756.90	113.10	13	3	37.70
5	120.00	91.20	28.80	24	1	28.80
6	130.00	100.10	29.90	23	2	14.95
7	680.00	605.20	74.80	11	3	24.93
8	1,720.00	1,599.60	120.40	7	7	17.20
9	1,960.00	1,842.40	117.60	6	8	14.70
10	5,160.00	5,005.20	154.80	3	4	38.70
Total	13,160.00	12,066.80	1,093.20	8.3	40	27.33

"In the table, we can see that the levels of gross profits are very wide, ranging from 3% to 24%. The average gross profit is about 8%, and average gross profit per item is $27.33. The consumer product range is very sensitive to the prices, and in previous years the company used different discount programs to boost sales, which from one side can increase the turnover but from another side can decrease company gross profit.

"Invoices 9 and 10 represent one of our discount programs; as a result, we had small gross profit but big turnover. Also, the company was selling out the old products from our stock by means of reducing price. This action helped us to decrease stock expenses and increase turnover, but the gross profit on these sales was not very high. Invoice 8 represents the selling out of old models."

Professional Products

Table 23.13-2. Invoice Analysis: Sales of Professional Products

Number	Invoice Price ($) A	Goods or Materials at Cost Price ($) B	Gross Profit ($) C = (A − B)	Gross Profit (%) D = (C ÷ A)	Number of Items E	Average Gross Profit per Item ($) F = (C ÷ E)
1	1,020.00	734.40	285.60	28	2	142.80
2	1,560.00	1,138.80	421.20	27	3	140.40
3	320.00	224.00	96.00	30	1	96.00
4	540.00	399.60	140.40	26	1	140.40
5	2,060.00	1,648.00	412.00	20	4	103.00
6	1,544.00	1,188.88	355.12	23	2	177.56
7	680.00	476.00	204.00	30	2	102.00
8	890.00	631.90	258.10	29	2	129.05
9	3,300.00	2,673.00	627.00	19	5	125.40
10	2,800.00	2,380.00	420.00	15	4	105.00
Total	14,714.00	11,494.58	3,219.42	22	26	123.82

"Professional products are more expensive than consumer products and the gross profit is also higher. The reason is that all consumer goods are sold from shops, whereas professional products need to be demonstrated, requiring additional expenses, managerial qualification, and effort. In the table we can also see that the level of gross profits range from 15% to 30%. The results of this are games with discount in order to boost sales.

Spare Parts

Table 23.13-3. Invoice Analysis: Sales of Spare Parts

Number	Invoice Price ($) A	Goods or Materials at Cost Price ($) B	Gross Profit ($) C = (A − B)	Gross Profit (%) D = (C ÷ A)	Number of Items E	Average Gross Profit per Item ($) F = (C ÷ E)
1	13.00	7.80	5.20	40	3	1.73
2	140.00	84.00	56.00	40	20	2.80
3	8.40	5.04	3.36	40	2	1.68
4	5.60	3.64	1.96	35	1	1.96
5	56.00	36.96	19.04	34	4	4.76
6	78.00	51.48	26.52	34	10	2.65
7	123.00	86.10	36.90	30	12	3.07
8	3.600	2.52	1.08	30	1	1.08
9	95.00	61.75	33.25	35	15	2.22
10	155.00	108.50	46.50	30	25	1.86
Total	677.60	447.79	229.81	34	93	2.47

"We can see that the average gross profit margin spare part is 34%, which is obviously higher than in selling consumer and professional goods. The company understands that in the current economic climate, a customer will prefer to repair the old than pay for new equipment.

"Based on this prediction, the company expected an increase in selling spare parts and decided to increase the price accordingly with a resulting increase in gross profit contribution, where we see a fluctuation of from 30% to 40% due to discounting.

"The invoice analyses show me that all three segments are heading in totally different directions from the company's official position relating to gross profit contribution, gross profit margin percentage, gross profit per item, and pricing policy in general.

"Based on that, I find it very important that management redesign our current reporting system in order to see separate reports on each of the three product segments. I see that is also very important that an individual target average rate index—TARI—be established as a benchmark for each segment in order to compare the received result with TARI at weekly intervals, and if necessary provide preventive action.

"Based on these analyses, I would be able to more constructively allocate marketing expenses and create a new price discount policy separately for each grouping."

23.14 Commercial Vehicle Sales

Nick Bronsen is the marketing manager for BBB, a company importing commercial vehicles and overseeing their sales through the dealers' network. In addition, the company provides spare parts, after-sales service, and sales of used trucks.

Nick analyzed 10 representative invoices in Table 23.14-1.

Table 23.14-1. Invoice Analysis of 10 Vehicle Sales

Number	Invoice Price (Net of Tax) ($) A	Cost of Goods Sold ($) B	Gross Profit C = (A − B)	Gross Profit (%) D = (C ÷ A)	Number of Items E	Average Gross Profit per Item (C ÷ E)
A*38/	22,350	18,707	3,643	16.30	1	3,643
A*77/	38,728	32,420	6,308	16.29	2	3,154
A*72/	89,820	74,828	14,992	16.69	4	3,748
A*81/	23,617	18,501	5,116	21.66	1	5,116
A*85/	22,525	18,707	3,818	16.95	1	3,818
A*92/	20,470	16,184	4,286	20.94	1	4,286
A*89/	58,551	48,585	9,966	17.02	3	3,322
A*97/	30,323	27,567	2,756	9.09	1	2,756
A*83/	55,415	50,855	4,560	8.23	1	4,560
A*80/	59,557	55,765	3,792	6.37	1	3,792
Total	421,356	362,119	59,237	14.06	16	3,702

"The annual gross profit margin taken from the accounts is 14.55%.

"The average value of the sample invoices is 14.06%. The difference is 0.49%, or in percentage terms 3.4%. So our result deriving from 10 invoices is close to being representative and serves our purpose."

Gross Profit per Sale

"In the Invoice Analysis, we see that levels of profitability are quite different. Analyzing this situation I found the following main reasons:

- "Profit depends significantly upon the range of vehicle. For example, invoice A*80/, with minimum level of gross profit 6.37%, refers to the sale of a heavy truck. At the same time, this invoice has one of the highest unit price, whereas absolute value of gross profit of $3,792 corresponds to $3,818 of invoice A*85/07 with gross profit % equal to 16.95%.

- "Profitability also depends upon the type of buyer. There are sales to the dealers, but there are also sales to the final customers, mainly owners of big fleets, and key accounts. Discounts to the clients are significantly lower than discounts given to the dealers. It corresponds to the difference in profitability equal to 4.5% of gross profit %. As an example, we could look at invoices A*81/ and A*85/."

Suggestions for Financial Planning and Existing Corporate Software

"On the basis of the analysis, we have seen that profitability of the company is subjected to several important parameters: types of products, levels of discounts, et cetera.

"The difference in gross profit performance per sale can be very high in absolute and percentage value. In such a situation, it becomes very important to carry out a correct commercial policy, taking into consideration market opportunities, dealer activity, and desirable profitability of the company.

"For financial planning, I would suggest changing our current approach to the basic information and reporting system.

"Right now we make two kinds of budgets: commercial people plan unit and model sales, whereas financial people plan annual gross profit (AGP).

"In general, commercial people do not care about AGP, and financial people do not care about units and models. It is clear that such a situation is misleading. That is why I would suggest modifying the existing planning system and developing new software, which could give us a possibility to plan our activity as a whole."

"The useful and logic solution could be implementation of Contribution-Based Activity with corresponding Target Average Rate Indexes. The CBA is able to establish capacity utilization along with an overview of contribution of services, products, and customers, in a matter of minutes from a sample of invoices."

Comment

These 14 "findings" highlight the value of reviewing and analyzing a representative sample of invoices.

Each participant saw added value in establishing a target average rate index (TARI) as a basis for pricing and monitoring output.

In each case, the insights gained pointed to a need for more relevant feedback from existing information systems.

Several of the preceding 22 chapters have pointed to the importance of what amounts to a "keyhole" view of a business, by means of an invoice analysis. We have also seen that the insight gained is but the first step on the road to putting CBA/TARI concepts into play. The hard part is sustaining a disciplined follow-through to make it happen.

APPENDIX A

Questions Answered

With the exception of matters relating to such topics as Absorption, Marginal, or Activity-Based Costing, this appendix attempts to respond in more detail to some of the many and varied questions raised during the reading of this book.[1]

It illustrates the following:

- Diagnosing problems
- Identifying productivity
- Establishing a TARI benchmark in manufacturing
- Achieving competitive advantage
- Establishing a TARI benchmark in retail
- Accuracy of sample using invoice analysis
- Sustaining competitive advantage
- Comparing actual results with target

---

[1] For those looking to compare CBA with systems such as Absorption Costing, Marginal Costing, or Time-Based ABC, the key difference lies in CBA's focus on tracking the targeted number of unit-contributions required to cover expenses plus profit. Costing systems focus on the accuracy of the unit cost and assume management will apply a markup percentage to cover profit.

Diagnosing Problems

Using a real-life case study, participants in accounting firm–sponsored workshops in several Western, English-speaking countries were invited to assume they were interviewing the manager of a print-jobbing firm in an attempt to diagnose the cause of his problem.

The manager said he was adding 25% to all jobs to cover profit, but had ended the past two years with less than a 5% net profit.

Presented with a summarized profit-and-loss trend (Table A-1), and assuming no change in work in progress or stock on hand, participants were asked to write out their initial diagnostic question.

Table A-1. XYCo: Profit & Loss Statement Period Ending _____

ITEM	Last Year $	%	This Year $	%
A. Sales	1,000,000	100	1,100,000	100
B. Materials	250,000	25	300,000	27
C. Gross Profit Contribution (A − B)	750,000	75	800,000	73
D. Wages	380,000	38	410,000	37
E. Other Expenses	370,000	37	390,000	35
F. Total Expenses (D + E)	750,000	75	800,000	73
G. Net Profit (C − F)	0	0	0	0

Of the 1,754 responses handed in:

- 1,262, or 72%, queried the increased level of expenses and asked for more details,
- 351, or 20%, queried the increased cost of materials and the level of markups,
- 88, or 5%, queried a variety of matters ranging from product mix to market competition, and
- 53, or 3%, queried the level of productivity and asked for staffing details.

Identifying Productivity

Asked what role they thought the level of productivity would play, there was general agreement that it would be an important factor, but given the information available, there was no way of identifying it, and nobody was aware of any simple cost-effective technique that would enable a comparison of actual output with input.

It was time to demonstrate such a technique. Using a representative sample of invoices, billed production hours were extracted from job sheets and analyzed as shown in Table A-2.

Table A-2. XYCo Invoice Analysis to Determine Average Contribution per Unit of Activity

Invoice Number	Invoice ($) A	Materials ($) B	Gross Profit ($) C = (A − B)	Gross Profit (%) C ÷ A	Hours Estimated or Quoted D	Average $ Gross Profit per Hour E = (C ÷ D)
148	1,312	345	967	74	12	81
163	944	287	657	70	11	60
119	2,175	587	1,588	73	41	39
105	188	55	133	71	3	44
137	475	119	356	75	4	89
152	3,617	1,048	2,569	71	54	48
Total	8,711	2,441	6,270	72	125	50

With a gross profit contribution of $800,000 for the most recent year and an average gross profit contribution of $50 per billed hour, it was possible to provide a close estimate of hours billed:

$$\text{Gross Profit Contribution} \quad \frac{\$800,000}{\$50.00} = 16,000 \text{ hours}$$

The printing firm employed 18 for hands-on production, which, with overtime, amounted to 36,000 hours available for charging to jobs.

$$\text{Productivity} \quad \frac{16,000 \text{ hours} \times 100}{36,000 \text{ hours}} = 44.44\%$$

8 hours × 44.44% = 3 hours, 33 minutes billed hours per day per production employee

It was apparent that if the business broke even at 44% productivity, billings at 60% productivity, using similar charge-out rates, could potentially result in an additional $280,000 contribution to the bottom line—less any additional variable costs such as power.

- (60% × 36,000 hours) = 21,600 hours
- (21,600 hours − 16,000 hours) = 5,600 hours
- (5,600 hours × $50) = $280,000

Knowing the level of productivity opens up the possibility of securing additional business at contribution rates lower than $50 and achieving a substantial profit.

Establishing TARI for a Manufacturing Business

The Invoice Analysis demonstrates the relationship between financial and physical "levers" of contribution[2] and productivity at play, the timely management of which is fundamental to profitable performance of any business, whatever its classification.

A significant advantage of this approach is the ability to start tracking actual results for comparison with a target (TARI—Target Average Rate Index) at the outset, without the need to spend time analyzing past results.

Unfortunately for business in general, current commercial software does not make it easy to relate the contributions flowing from an invoice with the relevant units of activity in order to demonstrate unit-contribution for comparison with TARI. Rather, invoicing systems extract typical invoice data from financial files that remain separate from the job files in management accounts.

As a result, extensive management feedback reports, covering variances from target in productivity and material usage, normally presented well after the month to which the data refers, tend to play little part in the daily business of quoting and pricing.

Yet at the time of quoting, pricing, or invoicing, knowing whether a contribution is above or below a target contribution can prove instrumental to survival and profitable performance.

The first step is to establish a benchmark, and for this we will use a jobbing company, HICo (Table A-3).

---

[2]Gross profit contribution = sales less materials or goods at cost. Also referred to simply as *contribution*.

Table A-3. Jobbing Company HICo Develops a TARI Benchmark

A	Target Expenses	$1,000,000
B	Target Profit	$200,000
C = (A + B)	Target Contribution	$1,200,000
D	Target Billable Hours	20,000
E = (C ÷ D)	Target Average Contribution per Hour TARI	$60

In order to emphasize its statistical status as a benchmark, target average contribution is referred to as the target average rate index.

Comparing the contribution per hour of an invoice with a TARI of $60 (Table A-4) raises the question as to how the outcome could have been improved at the time of quoting.

Table A-4. HICo Compares Job No. 143 with TARI

Invoice Number	Invoice ($) A	Materials ($) B	Contribution ($) C = (A − B)	Contribution (%) D = (C ÷ A)	Units (Hours) E	Average Contribution per Hour F = C ÷ E	TARI
143	7,600	2,000	5,600	74	120	$47	$60

Could the work have been done in 100 hours rather than 120? Could materials be acquired at a better price than $2,000—say, for $1,800?

One thing is for sure: it is not possible to improve on an unknown, so if the unit contribution of an invoiced sale cannot be compared with its TARI equivalent, it is unlikely there will be any change for the better.

Achieving Competitive Advantage

Important as it is to compare the average unit contribution[3] of a job with TARI, it is equally important to do so in full knowledge of the total contribution of all jobs invoiced in the target period.

This means recording billings so that the total contribution as well as the average unit contribution can be compared with target on an accumulative basis. Table A-5 provides an example of HICo a few weeks down the track.

---

[3]In the manufacturing/jobbing/service sectors, a unit will normally be a production-hour.

Appendix A | Questions Answered

Table A-5. HICo Compares Actual with Target for Weeks Ending _____

Invoice Number	Invoice ($) A	Materials ($) B	Contribution ($) C = (A − B)	Gross Profit (%) C ÷ A	Units (No. Hours) D	Average per Unit ($) E = (C ÷ D)
148	1,312	382	930	71%	19	49
163	944	330	614	65%	8	77
119	2,175	652	1,523	70%	28	54
105	188	62	126	67%	2	63
152	5,549	1,997	3,552	64%	57	62
Total	10,168	3,423	6,745	66%	114	59
Weeks to date	120,000	39,600	80,400	67%	1,386	58
Total to date	130,168	43,023	87,145	67%	1,500	58
Target	128,500	42,405	86,095	67%	1,435	60
Variance	+1,668	+618	+1,050	0%	+65	−2

Results to date show HICo is $1,050 ahead of target contribution and billing 65 more hours at a rate very close to the TARI of $60.

The company is in a position to get a foot in the door of a desirable customer by intentionally underquoting, in the knowledge that it:

a) Can afford to underquote by up to $1,500 without impacting target contribution,

b) Has the advantage over a competitor of knowing where it stands in relation to its bottom line when quoting.

Simple as it is, achieving competitive advantage calls for the discipline involved in identifying and tracking billed output weekly and accumulatively. Because current commercial software, driven largely by traditional accounting methodology, does not seamlessly connect the invoiced amount with the unit of activity (a billed production-hour in the case of HICo), it will be necessary to input the connection manually or develop software to do it.

Establishing a TARI for a Retail Business

Similar methodology applies in RTCo, a hypothetical retail or wholesale outlet, where sales are priced by marking up the cost of goods sold. In order to meet the desired profit for a given period, the retail outlet will need to make as many sales as necessary to provide the overall contribution needed to cover in-house expenses plus profit.

The targeted number of sales will be confined to the capacity of staff to handle throughput. Interfirm comparison data provides an indication of productivity levels for the type of outlet—such as gross sales per staff member or a target of four sales an hour (Table A-6).

Table A-6. Retailer RTCo Develops a TARI Benchmark

A	Target Expenses in Retail	$100,000
B	Target Profit	$20,000
C = (A + B)	Target Contribution	$120,000
D	Target Number of Sales	8,000
E = (C ÷ D)	Target Average Contribution per Sale	$15
F = (C ÷ D)	Target Average Rate Index (TARI)	$15

Sales for a day or a week can then be compared with TARI (Table A-7).

Table A-7. RTCo. Invoice Analysis of Retail Department for Comparison with TARI

Sales ($) A	Cost of Goods Sold ($) B	Contribution ($) C = (A − B)	Gross Profit (%) D = (C ÷ A)	Units (Number of Sales) E	Average Contribution per Sale($) F = (C ÷ E)	TARI ($)
3,000	2,000	1,000	33%	100	$10	$15

Undershooting TARI by $5 a sale indicates the need to review what is happening on the shop floor. Is markup being correctly applied? Is discounting taking place? What stock is the store promoting at the expense of the more profitable items?

In the case of retail, where software is programmed to reveal the unit[4] contribution as a percentage to sale, there is the same absence of perceived need to compare the unit financial contribution with a target, whether singly per transaction or accumulatively by the day or week.

As data is built up day by day or week by week, the invoice analysis will provide a summary of sales that allows one to compare the average contribution per sale with TARI as well as the number of sales with target. Table A-8 provides an example.

---

[4] In retail, a *unit* refers to an invoiced sale or a cash ring-up.

Table A-8. RTCo. Retail Sales Analysis for Weeks Ending _____

Sample Day or Week	Sales ($) A	Cost of Goods ($) B	Contribution ($) C = (A − B)	Gross Profit (%) C ÷ A	Number of Sales/Cash Ring-Ups D	Average Contribution per Sale ($) E = (C ÷ D)
1	1,454	974	480	33	30	16
2	3,900	2,808	1,092	28	78	14
3	635	419	216	34	12	18
4	1,397	992	405	29	27	15
5	1,714	1,234	480	28	24	20
6	2,969	2,018	951	32	50	19
Total	12,069	8,445	3,624	30	221	16
Target	11,136	7,461	3,675	33	245	15
Variance	+933	+984	−51	−3	−24	+1

Contribution percentage on cost of goods is 3 percentage points below target, possibly due to discounting or inadequate markup; the number of sales is also down 24 from target. The good news is that the sales are $933 higher than target, resulting in an average contribution greater than target, suggesting more aggressive salesmanship, improved product mix, or maybe pruning lower-priced items from the inventory.[5]

Where sufficient data is available, the analysis can be broken down by product, department, or representative, as demonstrated in Table A-9.

Table A-9. Example of Customer, Product, or Representative Analysis

Sales for Period xyy	Sales ($) A	Cost of Goods ($) B	Gross Profit ($) C = (A − B)	Gross Profit (%) C ÷ A	Sales Invoiced D	Average Gross Profit per Sale ($) E =(C ÷ D)
Customer 1	6,080	4,074	2,006	33	80	25
Customer 2	4,750	3,420	1,330	28	78	17
Product A	1,510	950	560	37	23	24
Product B	3,180	2,571	609	19	41	15
Rep 1	20,459	14,116	6,343	31%	373	17
Rep 2	24,354	18,509	5,845	24%	308	19

[5] The jeweler in Chapter 8 summarizes his reasons for improved performance.

Accuracy of Sample Using Invoice Analysis

The reaction of a client viewing hourly contributions ranging from $40 to $89 as in XYCo (Table A-2) is invariably one of surprise if not shock, and the question arises as to whether such a small sample of invoices could provide a reasonably accurate representation of the whole—particularly in the case of high- and low-value products or departments/branches involved in different activities.

While the selection of a "representative" sample is rightfully subject to criticism as being highly subjective, inputting more invoices can easily dispel concerns about the reliability of data.

Use of a representative sample of invoices to identify actual output for comparison with input, checked for reliability,[6] has proven to be an effective diagnostic tool, applicable across the spectrum of business categories from manufacturing, trades, contracting, and hospitality to the service professions.

In the case of a business marketing high- as well as low-value products, experience suggests that in the first instance, it is enough to take a sample across the range and review whether a more departmentally specific approach would have greater relevance.

For example, in a business with several branches and invoices ranging in price from $100 to $100,000, the average contribution of $6,000 is purely a statistic, but is nevertheless a basis upon which each branch could begin the process of tracking and improving the branch average contribution per sale.

Sustaining Competitive Advantage

Given increased output because of an improved level of productivity, can the average contribution per unit of output be sustained in a competitive market?

As we have seen, the average contribution is the average of a range of contributions. Awareness of such a range invariably prompts a search for ways and means of maximizing the highs and minimizing the lows.

---

[6]Reliability, or confidence level, can be checked by comparing the contribution percentage of the sample with the percentage in the profit-and-loss statement, or by comparing the average contribution of the sample with the overall average contribution obtained by dividing total contribution by the total number of invoices.

In the case of XYCo, the unit average gross profit contribution of $50 revealed in the invoice analysis (Table A-2) reflects the pricing and productivity of past performance in which output rated 44% or 16,000 hours out of a potential 36,000 hours. Looking ahead to an improved performance in output, the question arises as to whether the average of $50 per unit is sustainable in the event of targeting say, 20,000 billable hours?

As we saw in the case of Job 143 in Table A-4, in cases where the quoted gross profit contribution per hour of $47 falls below a TARI of $60, production times and/or the cost of materials would be reassessed. A manager in conjunction with the supervisor could work out ways and means of completing the job in closer to 100 hours:

(120 hours × $47) = $5,640. (100 hours × $60) = $6,000.

It is this step-by-step approach to quoting and pricing in conjunction with tracking actual hours charged and billed to jobs on a week-by-week basis that begins to impact the bottom line, slowly at first and then quite dramatically. For example, in Table A-10, using a TARI of $50 based on 400 billed hours a week, we compare actual results with target actual after 5 weeks.

Table A-10. Monitoring Results: 5-Week Comparison with Target

Item	Contribution ($)	Units (Hours) Billed	Average Unit Contribution ($)
Period to Date (5 weeks)	105,000	1,842	57
Target	100,000	2,000	50
Variance	+5,000	−158	+7

Now let's look at the 10-week period in (Table A-11).

Table A-11. Monitoring Results: 10-Week Comparison with Target

Item	Contribution ($)	Units (Hours) Billed	Average Unit Contribution ($)
Period to Date (10 weeks)	215,000	3,644	59
Target	200,000	4,000	50
Variance	+15,000	−356	+9

Improving Profit

The overall contribution is ahead due to an increase in the unit contribution, while units of activity have yet to reach target. It demonstrates a general rule that it is easier to improve unit contribution than overall productivity; the latter invariably requires more time. In other words, focusing on improving work method and efficiency per job can improve the the contribution for the job. But improving billed output overall calls for scheduling of job throughput with minimum of delay between jobs—a process that doesn't happen overnight.

APPENDIX B

Fast-Track Problem Resolution Guide

	Chapter #
Cash drying up?	6, 10, 21
Marketing in need of support?	7, 11, 13
Jobs profitable, but net profit poor?	3, 12
Working "flat-out" and getting nowhere?	6, 10, 19
Starting up a business?	8, 9
Planning for the next period?	9, 11
Checking profitability of product or job?	2, 3, 11
Losing out on quotes?	5, 11, 17
Buying—or merging—an existing business?	7, 11, 12
Need to cull some products?	4, 13

Appendix B | Fast-Track Problem Resolution Guide

Setting charge rates in a professional practice?	14, 15, 16
Establishing an incentive system?	5, 15
Want to get a foot in the door of a big customer?	3, 11
Competition proving strong?	4, 11, 17
Problem with pricing?	6, 20, 21
Looking for more profitable products?	11, 13, 18
Can't get new ideas implemented?	22
Want to check staff productivity?	8, 10, 21
Targeting and achieving net profit?	3, 8, 9, 10
Want to improve feedback?	8, 12
Relying on time sheets?	5, 14
Difference between productivity and efficiency	16, 19

APPENDIX C

Definition of Terms

Activity refers to the key activity fundamental to and driving all other activities. It can be the billed production-hours[1] or minutes, number of sales, meals (covers) served, tons per mile, skins tanned, and so forth.

Actual vs. Potential refers to the actual output of a business compared with its potential output, given the available resources of personnel, equipment, and technology.

Added Value refers to the amount added to the cost of materials/goods toward covering expenses plus profit. Applied as an add-on to cost of materials/goods, it is also referred to as **Gross Profit** or Gross Profit Contribution or, simply, **Contribution.**

Average Rate Index (ARI) refers to the average of units of activity derived from analyzing past performance. It is historical fact, not targeted. (See **Target Average Rate Index**.)

Capacity refers to the output potential of a business. For example, "At 80% of capacity, the business produces 8,000 widgets," meaning that at 100% capacity, the business is capable of producing 10,000 widgets.

Chargeable Activity is the same as billed or **Invoiced Activity**.

Contribution refers to the amount added to the cost of materials/goods toward covering expenses plus profit. Total contribution for a period, divided by planned or targeted number of units of activity, results in a target average

---

[1] A production-hour (or minute, etc.) only becomes an effective unit of activity if it is billable. In other words, a unit of activity makes no contribution to the bottom line unless it is billed.

Appendix C | Definition of Terms

contribution per unit—known as **target average rate index (TARI)**, to emphasize that it is a benchmark against which quoted or priced unit-contributions can be measured or compared.

Efficiency of an action or a process will impact productivity. A business can increase productivity by improving the work method and reducing the time involved in carrying out an activity. (Chapter 19 provides a good example).

Gross Profit in this book refers to the margin between sales and cost of goods or materials. It is often referred to as **Contribution** or **Added Value**. There is no universal agreement on the definition of gross profit. In manufacturing and similar businesses, it is frequently defined as sales less (cost of materials + factory-on, or variable, costs). Can also be defined as expenses + profit, where expenses and profit refer to operational expenses and profit and exclude cost of goods or materials and outsourced work.

Invoice/Invoice Activity is the same as billing; it refers to the amount charged out to customers. Tax is excluded when analyzing invoices or billings.

Net Profit refers to the bottom line after all operational and nonoperational income and expenditure is accounted for.

On-Costs refers to costs that are added on such as rent, power, depreciation, and so forth.

Output Activity refers to the units of key activity, such as hours, minutes, number of sales, meals (covers), or room-nights, that can be charged and invoiced. It is often referred to as "productive or billed units of activity" as compared with "available units of activity."

Profit refers to the bottom line, or what is left over after all operational income and expenses are accounted for.

Productivity refers to output, measurable as billed units of output as a percentage of available units of output. The more efficient the process, the more the output per unit of input.

Rate is short for the gross profit per unit of output activity.

Revenue is sales by another name, often used by professional businesses that bill fees.

Target Average Rate refers to the average gross profit contribution per unit of output activity that has been planned as a target benchmark. See **Average Rate Index (ARI)**.

Target Average Rate Index (TARI) is the same as Target Average Rate, but with *Index* added to emphasize its status as a benchmark and not a cost to be applied.

Unit refers to a single unit of output activity such as a production- (person) or machine-hour or minute, a sale, a meal (cover), a ton per mile, and so forth.

The Business Wheel

A wheel that operates around a well-maintained hub (Figure D-1), with spokes of even length and at even tension, is far more likely to perform in a balanced state than a wheel with uneven spokes under varying tension that put undue pressure on the hub.

Figure D-1. The Business Wheel with well-balanced spokes. TARI = Target Average Rate Index (Target Average Gross Profit Contribution per unit of Targeted Output Activity[1]). *Contribution* refers to gross profit (or added value) calculated as sales less cost of goods or materials used.

---

[1]*Output activity* refers to physically measurable units of key activity traceable in output, like minutes, hours, number of sales, meals (covers), tons, kilometers, cans of beans, and the like.

Appendix D | The Business Wheel

Lacking awareness or feedback on what really drives the hub of business, the great majority of business wheels remain elliptical, resulting in stress on all parts. This occurs when one department pulls ahead of the others. For example, maybe marketing gains orders at a discount with special credit arrangements. That puts pressure on supply, cash flow, and the bottom line. Or production races ahead of demand and fills the warehouse with expensive inventory, putting pressure on marketing, purchases of materials, and cash flow.

Such actions inevitably impact the hub of a wheel targeted to cover a certain distance (gross profit contribution) at an average speed (TARI).

Check Your Wheel!

After explaining to 12 senior managers how various departments act as spokes around a hub, I asked them to view their businesses in a wheel format, grading each departmental spoke on a 1–10 scale and joining the points together.[2]

The illustrations speak for themselves (Figure D-2).

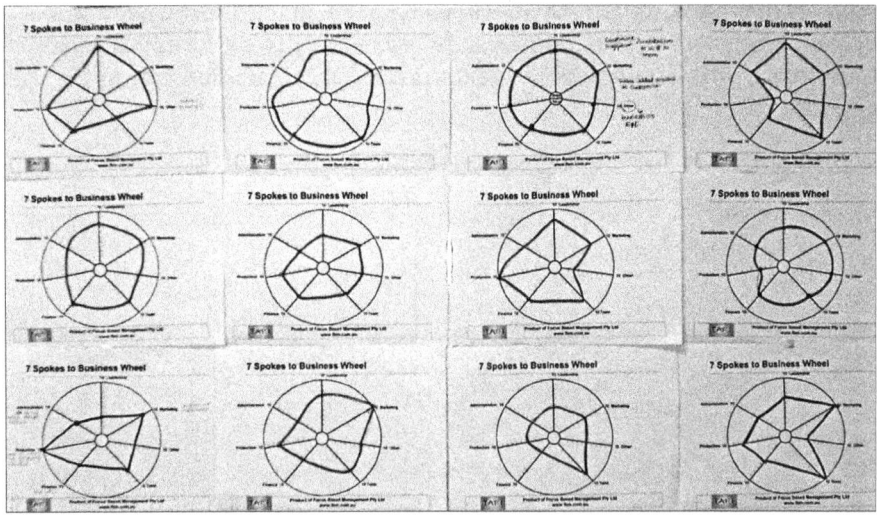

Figure D-2. Uneven spokes result in businesses that don't roll smoothly into the market

---

[2] A preceding exercise conducted with this group called for the spokes to be labeled a little differently from the pie chart in Figure D-1, but the essential idea remains.

Participants in the exercise headed up various functional departments such as finance, production, marketing, and human resources, which would have influenced their ratings to some degree. For example, the production executive would be likely to favor production over marketing and vice versa. Even so, extraneous economic factors aside, a balanced performance points to a meaningful correlation between a profitably performing hub and spokes under equal tension.

EPILOGUE

Epilogue: Why Contribution Metrics?

As a young man, I loved heading down to the sea in ships that made their way to distant ports of the world to trade cargoes of many kinds. Once we were clear of the noise, smells, pollution, and turmoil of port and out to sea, a smooth and steady rhythm settled upon the ship. Leaving loved ones behind, we went about our duties dulled by sweet sorrow until awaking like new beings to the movement of long swells beneath the keel, albatross soaring on a gentle breeze, and luminous stars in a clear sky.

An influence stronger than the sea drew me ashore where, like a fish out of water, I floundered in a strange and hostile environment. Someone said, "Study accounting by correspondence," and that is what I did, disliking the subject so much that I worked all hours to qualify in record time.

Once qualified as a CPA, the college asked me to take on the job of a state principal. I quickly accepted and in my enthusiasm for the course, I enrolled a record number of students—so many that the CEO asked me to explain my methods to the other principals. When they discovered I had nothing to impart about techniques of marketing or salesmanship, but was merely operating out of enthusiasm, their ballooning interest deflated.

Seeking truth, I studied all the subjects in philosophy and political science, qualifying with a bachelor of arts degree and a Commonwealth Government prize. Truth still elusive, I signed on for a thesis on the subject of Jean-Jacques

Rousseau's political obligation and the general will. Upon completing the thesis and getting no closer to truth with an MA in philosophy, I joined an international consulting group, hoping at least to find the truth about big business.

I learned that big business was in most cases an amalgam of branches or departments, and that success within a business had as much to do with nepotism and politics as competence.

Responding to the call for those with practical as well as academic qualifications, I took on a role as senior lecturer in accounting and business studies in a university offering degrees "similar to but different from" traditional universities. The university gained a reputation for graduating "practically oriented" students, and I became head of school, developing contacts with businesses locally and nationally. In those days, corporate planning was the flavor of the month and we were able to get the attention and active participation of CEOs of major industries in the first Corporate Planning Conference held in the country.

Offered a foundation chair as professor and head of the Department of Accounting and Business Studies at the University of Technology in Papua New Guinea (PNG), I signed a five-year contract. Once I was in situ, the position opened up active participation with the United Nations Committee on Small Business Development in South East Asia, and I was invited to join the country's National Economic Advisory Council.

In an attempt to reconcile the significant differences between a Western-driven approach to business development with local cultural attitudes, I completed a PhD on a strategy for small business development in PNG.

The end of the contract coincided with the need for our son to attend high school, so my family relocated to a research position in a university town back in Australia. The research focused on small-medium enterprises, and it was here that I came to see what we were teaching in accounting and finance had little relevance to the management decision-making needs of business in general, small or large. How best to identify and then resolve those needs was to absorb my time and energy in the years ahead.

In the process, I came to see that business was as much a part of the mainstream of life as art, science, sports, or philosophy. It provides food to eat, facilities to communicate, transport for trade and travel, gas, electricity, water, houses, and hospitals. It can be likened to a bloodstream, sustaining life as we know it on this planet, with shortage and starvation arising from natural or artificial blockages.

I saw that failure of a business follows a long period of stress for owners, managers, and families; for staff and their families; for unpaid suppliers and their families; and, to a lesser degree, the surrounding community. Moreover, I saw the cumulative effect of many failures influencing the medical, social, economic, and spiritual well-being of a nation. I saw millions upon millions of dollars raised in search of cures for cancer, but little research into the malignancy of problems at work and in business as a prime source of cancer in the human body.

Conversely, I saw how the success of a business, arrived at by honest endeavor and competent management, does more for the well-being of a nation than any tonic medicine has been able to devise.

Improving Profit: Using Contribution Metrics to Boost the Bottom Line is the author's contribution to the success of business.

Index

A

Activity, definition, 207
Added value, 207
Advertising expenditure, 136
Air conditioning units
   cost of, 122
   installation contractors
      commercial unit cost, 121
      equipment, 123
      hourly charge rates, 122
      hourly rate, 122
      low rate, 122
      manufacturer's method, 122
      TARI approach, 122–123
Assembly process, 136
Average contribution per hour, 150
Average gross profit vs. gross profit per man-hour, 172
Average rate index (ARI), 207
Average sale contribution
   contribution margin, 52
   discount, 52
   net profit, 53
   per sale, 56
   pricing, 52
   weekly basis, 51

B

Billable hours contribution
   Action Sheet, 73
   annual contribution, 72
   contribution-based activity, 74
   monthly feedback, 74
Budget, 151
Business, 153
   actual vs. potential, 207
   billable hours, 125
   contribution, 125
   reduction in, 151
   salon software, 153
   traditional approach, 125

C

Capacity, definition, 207
Cash flow, 147
CEO, 136
Chargeable activity, 207
Contribution, 125, 143, 151
   definition, 207
   hourly charge rate, 124–125
   track hours, four-month period, 146
Contribution-based activity (CBA), 74, 121, 138
   action meeting, 9
   application, 2
   automobile distribution, 182
   banking, 179
   engineering and design, 171
   farming equipment, 185
   household equipment, 184
   importing and distributing products, 187
   large-scale distribution, 167
   manufacturing and distribution, 166

Contribution-based activity (CBA) (cont.)
    packaging, 177
    real estate, 173
    sample invoice analysis, 7
    small and medium-sized businesses, 2
    software development, 169
    summary feedback report, 8
    TARI, 5
    unit contribution of invoiced transaction, 8
    vehicle manufacturing, 164
    vehicle sales, 190
Contribution per hour, 131
Contribution per man-hour, 129, 133
Contribution per unit, 143
Costing system, 23
Customer service
    feedback on, 154
    monitor progress, 152

D

Direct costs, 4, 93
Discounting, 61

E

Efficiency, definition, 208
Employee wages, 149
Estimating productivity, 151

F

Fabrication process, 137, 139
    contribution, 139
    European counterparts, 138
    finance director, 137
    marketing director, 137
    scaled-down representation, 136
    window frame department, 139
Fast-track problem
        resolution guide, 205–206
Finance, 138
Financial statements, 16
50-hours-per-house approach, 147

G

Gross profit, 130, 143, 208
Gross profit contribution, 77, 79, 124, 138, 207
    Action Sheet, 59
    average contribution per hour, 13, 20
    average sales, 56, 60 (see also Average
            sale contribution)
    balance hours, 15
    billable hours (see Billable
            hours contribution)
    contribution per sale, 59
    contribution rate, 23
    cost cutting, 15
    costing system, 23
    definition, 12, 19, 44, 50, 56
    discounting, 61
    gross profit margin, 28
    identifying average rate per
            production hour, 27
    invoice analysis, 14
    KPI, 13, 56
    manufacturing information system, 16
    per production-hour per product, 27
    planning and targeting, 58
    pricing policy, 59
    production hour, 12, 14, 15, 24
    product mix, 59
    quoting (see Quoting)
    targeted net profit, 21
    TARI, 13, 16, 26, 57
    unit contribution, 30
    weekly feedback, 16
    weekly performance, 61
Gross profit per sale, 191

H

Hourly rates, 153
Human comfort level (HCL), 36

I, J

Indirect costs, 4
Invoice analysis
    average gross profit per
            production hour, 14

Index

definition, 15
declining profitability
    accountant, 84
    Action Sheet, 87, 89
    capital injection, 84
    contribution per
        production-hour unit, 85
    gross profit contribution, 85
    invoice analysis, 89
    line management, 88
    marketing manager, 84
    planning and targeting, 86
    price for job, 84
    production manager, 84
    productivity, 85
    quotations, 87
    quoted *vs.* actual times, 84
    recognition of interdependence, 89
    TARI, 86
    track against benchmark, 86–87
    unit-contribution, 89
Invoice/invoice activity, 208
IT departments, 138

K

Key performance indicators
    (KPIs), 2, 13, 56

L

Leasing cost, 130
Long-term promotional strategy, 138

M

Manufacturing information system, 16
Marketing department, 138
Markup, definition, 56

N

Nationwide corporation, 138
Net profit, 147
    definition, 208
    planning, 143

O

On-costs, 208
On-the-spot analysis, 150
Operational costs, 94
Output activity, 208
Overhead costs, 4
Overquoting, 36
Overtime, 35

P

Preassembly method, 138
Predesigned plans, 142
Pricing
    business aspects, 81
    contribution per unit of activity, 82
    cost of subcontractors, 77
    40 percent markup, 76
    gross profit contribution, 77, 79
    handling work flow, 77
    in-house productivity, 80
    invoice analysis, 82
    key to success, 81
    number of employees, 76
    productivity level, 76
    quoting, 75
    targeting unit-activity, 80
    TARI, 79
    unit-contribution, 78, 80
Production hours, 4, 12, 14–15, 20, 24, 27
    Action Sheet, 45
    average contribution *vs.* TARI, 44
    billable hours, 42
    capturing data per week, 46
    comparison of invoices, 46
    identifying billed hours, 41
    identifying productive activity
        levels, 43, 47
    invoice analysis, 44
    order book, 43
    paid hours calculation, 41
    planning, 45
    productivity, 42
    TARI, 45

Index

Productivity
    average hourly charge rate, 150
    definition, 208
    estimation, 145
    level of, 154
    supervisory hours per house, 145
Products sales, 132
Profit, definition, 208
Profitable product identification
    Action Sheet, 95
    annual contribution target, 97
    business intelligence system, 98
    contribution margin, 98
    contribution per representative, 97
    contribution rates per
        production hour, 95
    crumpets, 92–93, 95
    discounted pies, 96
    dough-splattered crew, 96
    factory cost, 93
    fresh-faced audit team, 98
    gross profit contribution per man-hour, 92
    inquiries, 99
    level of productivity, 98
    meat pies, 92–93, 96
    pastry-encrusted plant, 96
    productivity, 94
    sales target, 94
    TARI, 94
    wholesale price, 96
Profit analysis. *See* Gross
        profit contribution

Q

Quoting
    Action Sheet, 34, 38
    billable units of activity, 35
    contribution rate, 37
    human comfort level (HCL), 36
    incentive system, 37
    level of billable activity, 37
    overquoting, 36
    overtime, 35
    TARI, 34
    time sheets, 38
    unit contribution and material cost, 38

R

Rate, definition, 208
Retail price, selling output, 132
Retail sales, 129
Revenue, definition, 208

S

Sales
    Action Sheet, 131
    products sales, 132
Small-home market, 138
Supervision hours, 144
Supervisors, 146, 148
    bonus incentive, 146
    contribution value per hour, 148
    estimating, purchasing, and
        construction process, 146
    supervising construction, 147
    supervisory role, 147
    TARI, 147

T

Target average gross profit contribution
        per hour. *See* Target average
        rate index (TARI)
Target average rate, 208
Target average rate index (TARI), 5, 13, 16, 20,
        23–24, 26, 130–131, 138–139, 143
    Action Sheets, 153
    air conditioning units, 122–123
    in bank, 182
    daily and weekly performance, 152
    daily and weekly tracking, 154
    declining profitability, 86
    definition, 208
    planning and targeting
        performance, 144
    pricing, 79
    profitable product identification, 94
    production hours, 44–45
    quoting, 34
    supervisors, 146–147
    supervisory hours per house, 145
    target average contribution, 64

Index

target contribution
  average gross profit contribution, 64
  results, 66
  targeting annual number of covers, 64
  targeting average contribution, 64
  targeting daily average contribution, 65
  wage calculation, 103–104
Targeted net profit per partner
  last year's productivity, 110
  staff's participation, 110
  targeting billable hours and average fees for year ending, 109
  targeting gross revenue for year ending, 108
  time and charge rate per client with TARI, 112
  weekly billing, 111
Target profit, 152
TARI. See Target average rate index (TARI)
Total hours sold vs. actual production-hours paid, 173

U, V

Unit, definition, 20, 208
Unit contribution, 78, 128
Unit of activity, 16

W, X, Y, Z

Wage calculation
  Action Sheet, 105
  computerized time sheets, 106
  improving time-sheet system, 102
  job targeting, 104
  job tracking, 104
  planning and targeting performance, 103
  potential gross fees, 102
  reconciliation, 106
  scarcity of cash, 102
  TARI, 103–104
  time-sheet control, 101
  total revenue, 105
  weekly meeting, 104
Wholesale, 129
  analysis of, 129
  prices, 132
Window frame-making process, 136–137. See also Fabrication process
Work study, 136–137, 139

Get the eBook for only $10!

Now you can take the weightless companion with you anywhere, anytime. Your purchase of this book entitles you to 3 electronic versions for only $10.

This Apress title will prove so indispensible that you'll want to carry it with you everywhere, which is why we are offering the eBook in 3 formats for only $10 if you have already purchased the print book.

Convenient and fully searchable, the PDF version enables you to easily find and copy code—or perform examples by quickly toggling between instructions and applications. The MOBI format is ideal for your Kindle, while the ePUB can be utilized on a variety of mobile devices.

Go to www.apress.com/promo/tendollars to purchase your companion eBook.

All Apress eBooks are subject to copyright. All rights are reserved by the Publisher, whether the whole or part of the material is concerned, specifically the rights of translation, reprinting, reuse of illustrations, recitation, broadcasting, reproduction on microfilms or in any other physical way, and transmission or information storage and retrieval, electronic adaptation, computer software, or by similar or dissimilar methodology now known or hereafter developed. Exempted from this legal reservation are brief excerpts in connection with reviews or scholarly analysis or material supplied specifically for the purpose of being entered and executed on a computer system, for exclusive use by the purchaser of the work. Duplication of this publication or parts thereof is permitted only under the provisions of the Copyright Law of the Publisher's location, in its current version, and permission for use must always be obtained from Springer. Permissions for use may be obtained through RightsLink at the Copyright Clearance Center. Violations are liable to prosecution under the respective Copyright Law.

Other Apress Business Titles You Will Find Useful

Using Technology to Sell
London
978-1-4302-3933-8

Plan to Turn Your Company Around in 90 Days
Lack
978-1-4302-4668-8

The Employer Bill of Rights
Hyman
978-1-4302-4551-3

Tax Strategies for the Small Business Owner
Fox
978-1-4302-4842-2

Know and Grow the Value of Your Business
McDaniel
978-1-4302-4785-2

Tax Insight
Murdock
978-1-4302-6310-4

Firing at Will
Shepherd
978-1-4302-3738-9

CFO Techniques
Guzik
978-1-4302-3756-3

Metrics
Klubeck
978-1-4302-3726-6

Available at www.apress.com

GPSR Compliance

The European Union's (EU) General Product Safety Regulation (GPSR) is a set of rules that requires consumer products to be safe and our obligations to ensure this.

If you have any concerns about our products, you can contact us on

ProductSafety@springernature.com

In case Publisher is established outside the EU, the EU authorized representative is:

Springer Nature Customer Service Center GmbH
Europaplatz 3
69115 Heidelberg, Germany

www.ingramcontent.com/pod-product-compliance
Lightning Source LLC
LaVergne TN
LVHW040736250326
834688LV00031B/316